# Wales at War

Phil Carradice

Gomer

First Impression – 2003
Second Impression – 2005

ISBN 1 84323 321 5

This book was first published with the financial
support of the Welsh Books Council.

Printed in Wales at
Gomer Press, Llandysul, Ceredigion

# Contents

# Acknowledgments

The greatest thanks have to go to the men and women who so openly and so willingly spoke about their experiences during the Second World War. As a writer and historian I owe them a debt that is hard to quantify, let alone repay. I am grateful that they all granted permission for me to use their words in written format in this book.

Most of the photographs in this book were loaned by the men and women whose stories and lives they illustrate. To them, many thanks. Other photographs come from the author's own archive, from West Glamorgan Archive Service, from Chris S. Stephens and from the Opie collection.

Thanks also to Steve Groves of BBC Radio Wales for his enthusiasm and dedication – without him the task would have been impossible; to Geoff Ballinger and Ceri Davies of BBC Wales Education; to Mairwen Prys Jones of Gomer whose idea this was in the first place; to the members and officials of South Pembs Golf Club; to the staff of the Royal Monmouthshire Royal Engineers Museum; to the Vale of Glamorgan Library Service; to everyone who helped in any way with the project.

And last but not least to Trudy, who endured paper and books all over the house – and then ended up typing the manuscript when she would have much preferred beating me on the golf course.

# Introduction

The history of the Second World War has been told many times. Yet, often, what is related is either the story of the strategic war, the great campaigns and points of conflict, or the experiences of famous men like Churchill, Montgomery, Rommel or Eisenhower.

This book is different in that it is not, in the main, concerned with the lives of great generals or politicians. They undoubtedly shaped the conflict and decided on its course and conduct. However, the ordinary men, women and children – in the home, in the air-raid shelter, on merchant navy cargo ships or in factories and coalmines – are the focus for this study. The book is about them, their responses and feelings, their actions and deeds. It aims to give a true and accurate picture of what it was like to live through those dangerous years between 1939 and 1945.

The book is directly focussed on Wales. It is about ordinary Welsh people during the Second World War. While, in many respects, their experiences were similar to those of people from Coventry or Glasgow – and can, in fact, be taken as being representative of Britain as a whole – in many other ways, their experiences were very different. What they saw and felt was so particular, so uniquely Welsh, that the greatest wonder is simply that their stories have not been told before.

From the outset, let me declare a personal interest in the history of the Home Front in Wales during the Second World War. So much so that that when Mairwen Prys Jones of Gomer Press suggested this project I leapt at the chance to research, compile and write the book.

My uncle was Arthur Morris, the Pembroke Dock Fire Chief during the war. It was he who fought the momentous blaze when the Pembroke Dock oil tanks were bombed in 1940. Strangely, I knew next to nothing about his part in the affair until after his death in 1970. He would not speak about the bombing, no matter how many times I nagged him or my father or my other relations to tell me what happened to them during the war years.

Uncle Arthur was a modest man – one of the things that, I hope, will emerge from the recollections in this book. It was only when Vernon Scott published his fine account of the bombings (*Inferno* published by the *The Western Telegraph*, 1980) that I began to realize just what Arthur Morris and other firemen from the period had endured.

From that time began an abiding interest in the war – not the great campaigns or battles, but about how the conflict affected people living at home, working in shops and offices and turning out in their own time to fire-watch, to march with the Home Guard and to carry out those vital duties that were often ignored or taken for granted. That, really, is the crux of this book.

Firemen, ARP wardens, police officers and members of the Home Guard all played a vital role in defeating Hitler. So, too, did the men and women who worked in the mines and factories or, as Land Army Girls, in the fields and forests of Wales. Bevin Boys and merchant seamen who sailed out of Welsh ports like Milford Haven all played their part – as, in their own way (although they would probably abhor the suggestion) did the conscientious objectors whose moral stance would not let them take up arms against their fellow human beings.

Add in the Italian and German prisoners-of-war who were sent to camps and farms in Wales; include the evacuees who flocked here in their thousands from cities like Birmingham and London; consider the children of Welsh towns and villages for whom the war could suddenly change from pleasures like collecting shrapnel and the nose cones off shells to the terror and hurt of lost brothers and parents. Do that and you can quickly compile a vivid, dramatic picture of Wales at war.

This book is for all the nameless but necessary people who fought their own war, in whatever way they had to do it. This is the history of ordinary men and women locked into a conflict they did not want or need. This, then, is their story.

*Chapter One*

# The Onset and Progress of War

IN ORDER to put the memories and stories that follow into some sort of perspective, it is important to have an understanding of how the Second World War unfolded. The war is, after all, the over-arching canopy under which people lived their lives during those turbulent years. As so many of the memories of people are haphazard in their order – accurate and informative but, invariably, jumping ahead or backwards in time – it is essential to gain a clear insight into the chronology of the war. This chapter attempts to provide exactly that.

The Second World War began on 3rd September, 1939. Yet its origins predate the declaration by several years. Indeed, the seeds of conflict were sown as far back as the Treaty of Versailles in 1919, that ill-judged and vindictive peace settlement which ended the first great war of the twentieth century.

In post-war Germany, a country disarmed and rendered impotent by military and economic sanctions, the mood turned increasingly towards the extremes. The 1920s were marked by significant political unrest as the forces of the left and right fought pitched battles on the streets in order to gain precedence.

History records that Adolf Hitler and his Nationalist Socialist German Workers Party – parading their limited and dangerous ideology behind the banner of Aryan nationalism – eventually claimed victory in the street battles. It was not before a failed political coup in 1923, which saw Hitler temporarily imprisoned, that a decision was made by the Nazi party that power, when it came, should be achieved by the ballot box and not the gun.

That position of power was eventually attained in January 1933 when Hitler was elected Chancellor. Barely a month later, on 22nd February, the Reichstag, the German Parliament building, was set on fire and Hitler immediately blamed the Communists for the outrage. He outlawed the Communist party and imprisoned all the main left-wing leaders. Before long the National Socialist Party was the only legal political party in Germany and, with the passing of the Enabling Laws, Hitler was able to enact legislation without bothering with the irrelevancy of Parliament. Democracy in Germany had been utterly demolished.

Over the next seven years Germany prepared steadily but relentlessly for war. Compulsory military service was introduced in 1935 and, secretly, an air force (the Luftwaffe) was created. The production of guns, tanks and aircraft became the main industry of the country. Hitler knew he was breaking the Treaty of Versailles. His view was simply that it was an unjust treaty anyway and, besides, so feeble was the reaction to his territorial aggression that he became convinced that nobody in war-torn Europe was willing or able to call his bluff.

The Nazi Party promised a return to prosperity       Hitler Youth on the march.
and power. This German postcard from 1938
sums up the mood of the people: one people, one
empire, one leader.

The 1930s saw increasing belligerence from Germany. In 1936 the Rhineland, which had been de-militarised after the First World War, was re-occupied. France and Britain did nothing. Austria was annexed (the Anschluss as it was called) when German troops marched across the border on 12th March, 1938 and Austria became part of the greater German Empire. Again, France and Britain did nothing.

Gaining in confidence, Hitler turned his attention to Czechoslovakia and her industrial power base in cities like Pilsen. The Sudetenland, that part of Czechoslovakia where most of the German-speaking Czechs lived, had been pressing for a union with the mother country for some time. In September 1938, fuelled by Nazi agents, unrest in these areas flared up into open riot. With German troops massing on her borders, the Czech army mobilised. The British and French governments prevaricated, promised help but, ultimately, once again did nothing.

British Prime Minister Chamberlain flew to Munich where he and French Premier Daladier agreed to proposals presented to them by the Italian dictator, Mussolini, but, in reality, drawn up by Hitler. Chamberlain came back to Britain waving the document of friendship that Hitler had signed and proudly declaring that he had achieved 'peace in our time'.

Abandoned by France and Britain, the Sudetenland was promptly invaded by Germany and, with other portions of land parcelled out to Poland and Hungary, Czechoslovakia virtually ceased to exist as an independent state. Whether

Chamberlain really believed that he had secured peace is a moot point – what he did do, however, was obtain a brief period of time in which Britain could start serious rearmament.

After walking into the rump of Czechoslovakia in March 1939, Hitler next turned his attention to Poland. After the First World War, a narrow corridor of land had been taken from Germany and given to Poland, to provide the country with access to the sea. The port of Danzig, in the corridor, had been placed under the control of the League of Nations. Now Hitler demanded the return of Danzig and the Polish Corridor.

Hitler enters the Sudetenland.

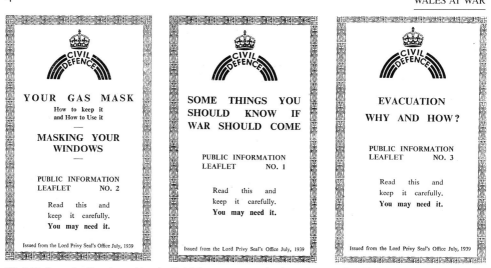

Civil Defence leaflets issued by the British government in the summer of 1939.

France and Britain, finally understanding that Hitler's lust for power knew no boundaries, vowed to defend Poland's sovereignty with military force. Reassured by a non-aggression pact with Russia, Hitler was aware that, in the short term at least, the threat from France and Britain was merely empty rhetoric. They were too far away to do little more than posture and protest. The only country that had the power, the will and the physical proximity to halt him was Russia and the treaty that his foreign minister von Ribbentrop had just signed with Stalin assured Hitler that the Russians would sit idly by as his tanks rolled towards Warsaw.

Poland was invaded on 1st September 1939. The following day Britain sent an ultimatum to Berlin, demanding withdrawal of German forces. It was ignored. On 3rd September, at 11.15 precisely, Prime Minister Chamberlain broadcast to the nation.

> 'This morning the British Ambassador handed the German Government a final note stating that unless we heard from them by 11.00 o-clock, that they were prepared at once to withdraw their troops from Poland, a state of war would exist between us. I have to tell you now that no such undertaking has been received and that, consequently, this country is at war with Germany.'

In Wales, like the rest of Britain, the announcement was greeted with horror and disbelief. Everyone had been aware of the crisis but no-one had wanted to believe it would come to this. MARY ROSE whose experiences are related in more detail in Chapter Three, remembers the moment, if not its magnitude, with great clarity:

> 'I remember it because it was a Sunday morning and my cousin Mair and I were on our way to chapel. The news came on, about the war, that we were at war with Germany, and I remember my mother and my aunt crying their eyes out. It didn't really affect us because we were so young. We didn't know what was happening.'

For others, slightly older, the news was more distressing. The RT REVEREND JOHN CLEDAN MEARS, former Bishop of Bangor, was an adolescent at the time. He remembers that

> 'I was sixteen years old when the war broke out. It cast a gloom everywhere. I was living on the west coast, in Cardiganshire, near Aberystwyth, and we used to hear planes going across. One began to feel, as perhaps they hadn't in previous generations, that now you were in the front line.'

Initially, however, little seemed to happen and, for most people in Wales, life went on as normal. Far away to the east, Poland was swiftly and easily conquered by the rampaging German army, cavalry charges against Panzer tanks proving that the old ways of war had finally gone forever. In Britain, however, despite an air raid warning following Chamberlain's message, bombs and poison gas did not immediately rain down on the populace. It was a case of 'Get on with your life'. If people had only known how quickly things were about to change.

## The Second World War – A Brief Chronology

10th September 1939    Lord Gort leaves for France with the first units of the British Expeditionary Force

14th October 1939    A German U-boat penetrates the defences of Scapa Flow and torpedoes the battleship *Royal Oak*. Nearly a thousand sailors lose their lives

8th November 1939    Hitler appoints Hans Frank Governor General of Poland. Under his brutal regime the persecution of European Jews begins to assume new and deadly heights.

Call up! Thousands of young men were called into the army once war was declared, many of them having to be housed in tents until more permanent accommodation could be found.

When the Germans attacked in May 1940, Britain and France were taken totally by surprise.

4th December 1939    King George VI visits soldiers of the BEF in France

13th December 1939   The Battle of the River Plate – *HMS Ajax*, *Achilles* and *Exeter* engage the pocket battleship *Graf Spee* off the coast of South America. Despite being severely damaged, the cruisers force *Graf Spee* to take refuge in Montevideo. Four days later she scuttles herself. It is the first British 'victory' of the war.

21st February 1940   Auschwitz concentration camp in Poland is opened. It will become the ultimate death camp.

9th April 1940       Germany invades Norway. Some British and German ships are sunk during the assault but by nightfall the German forces are ashore.

13th April 1940      The Battle of Narvik – eight German destroyers are sunk in Narvik fjord

9th May 1940         The German offensive in the west begins with a lightning assault on Belgium, Holland and Luxembourg.

10th May 1940        In Britain, Chamberlain resigns and is replaced as Prime Minister by Winston Churchill.

15th May 1940        Holland surrenders to the Germans.

16th May 1940        French and British troops begin to retreat in the face of lightning strikes by tanks and Stukka dive-bombers.

22nd May 1940        German forces reach the French coast, thus encircling the BEF. The army falls back to Dunkirk.

| 24th May 1940 | To the disgust of tank commanders like Rommel and Guderian, Hitler orders a halt to the advance on Dunkirk – Goering has assured him that the Luftwaffe will destroy the remnants of the BEF. |
| --- | --- |
| 27th May 1940 | An armada of 'little ships' from the south coast of England sails across the channel and begins to rescue the remnants of the BEF. |
| 3rd June 1940 | The last British, French and Belgian troops leave the Dunkirk beaches. Six hours later the German army enters the town. |
| 10th June 1940 | Italy declares war on Britain and France, Mussolini being keen to mirror the success of his fascist rival. |
| 22nd June 1940 | France signs an Armistice with Germany – in the same railway carriage where the armistice was signed in November 1918. Hitler cannot restrain his delight and does a little jig of victory. |
| 30th June 1940 | German troops land in the Channel Islands. It is the only piece of Britain that will be occupied during the war. |
| 10th July 1940 | The first German air raids are made on the south coast, thus beginning the Battle of Britain. |
| 16th July 1940 | Hitler issues Directive 16, setting out plans for the invasion of England – Operation Sea Lion. |
| 12th August 1940 | German dive-bombers attack radar stations along the south coast. |
| 15th August 1940 | More than 2000 sorties are flown over Britain by the Luftwaffe but the RAF holds steady. |
| 19th August 1940 | The oil tanks at Pembroke Dock are bombed, thereby creating the largest fire in Britain since 1666. |
| 7th September 1940 | Over 1000 German aircraft launch bombing raids on London. |
| 15th September 1940 | The RAF scrambles all its fighters to keep the enemy at bay – German losses are 56 aeroplanes, nearly a quarter of the attacking force. |
| 17th September 1940 | Hitler announces the postponement of Operation Sea Lion. The Battle of Britain has been won by the RAF. |
| 28th October 1940 | Italy invades Greece. The performance of the Italian army is so poor that, soon, Hitler has to reinforce them with German troops and planes. |
| 11th November 1940 | Swordfish aircraft of the Fleet Air Arm attack Taranto, sinking three Italian battleships. |

British forces in Egypt.

| 14th November 1940 | Coventry is bombed, nearly 1500 bombs falling on the city and severely damaging the cathedral. |
| 19th December 1940 | The Italians appeal to Hitler for troops to help them after several setbacks against British forces in North Africa. |
| 12th February 1941 | German commander Rommel arrives in Africa. |
| 7th March 1941 | The Battle of the Atlantic is now raging, with Allied merchant ships and German U-boats being sent to the bottom of the sea. |
| 24th March 1941 | With Allied forces being depleted to help defend Greece, Rommel starts to make swift gains against the British in North Africa. |
| 11th April 1941 | Tobruk is cut off and besieged by Rommel's forces. |
| 9th May 1941 | U110 is captured and a complete Enigma coding machine falls into British hands. It will enable experts to decipher German naval signals for the rest of the war. |
| 10th May 1941 | Rudolph Hess, deputy leader of the Nazi Party, flies to Britain in an attempt to broker a peace. He is imprisoned for the duration of the war. |
| 20th May 1941 | A German air assault by 20,000 paratroopers is launched on Crete. |

Winston Churchill kept up morale throughout the war with his speeches – as this 1940s postcard testifies.

The Spirit of Britain

WE SHALL GO ON TO THE END....WE SHALL FIGHT IN FRANCE, WE SHALL FIGHT ON THE SEAS AND IN THE OCEANS, SHALL FIGHT WITH GROWING CON-FIDENCE AND GROWING STRENGTH IN THE AIR.. WE SHALL DEFEND OUR ISLAND,WHATEVER THE COST MAY BE. WE SHALL FIGHT ON THE BEACHES,WE SHALL FIGHT ON THE LANDING GROUNDS, WE SHALL FIGHT IN THE FIELDS AND STREETS AND EVEN IN THE HILLS ....WE SHALL NEVER SURRENDER,AND EVEN IF, WHICH I DO NOT FOR A MOMENT BELIEVE,THIS ISLAND, OR EVEN PART OF IT,IS SUBJUGATED AND STARVING,THEN OUR EMPIRE ACROSS THE SEAS, ARMED AND GUARDED BY THE BRITISH FLEET, WILL CARRY ON THE STRUGGLE,UNTIL, IN GOD'S GOOD TIME,THE NEW WORLD, IN ALL ITS STRENGTH AND MIGHT, SETS FORTH TO THE RESCUE AND LIBERATION OF THE OLD. BRITAIN WILL FIGHT THE MENACE OF TYRANNY FOR YEARS, AND,IF NECESSARY, ALONE.
— WINSTON CHURCHILL

24th May 1941    HMS *Hood* is sunk by the *Bismarck*. The new battleship *Prince of Wales* is seriously damaged and has to withdraw from the action.

27th May 1941    Hunted down by Force H the *Bismarck* is disabled by torpedo bombers, battered by HMS *Rodney* and *King George V*. Torpedoes from British cruisers fail to sink her and eventually the German crew scuttle their mighty warship.

22nd June 1941    Germany invades Russia – Operation Barbarossa. There is no formal declaration of war and surprise is both immediate and effective. By midday over a thousand Russian aircraft have been destroyed and the German army has advanced over 40 miles into Russia. 'The great gamble' is underway, since Germany is now fighting the war on two fronts.

9th July 1941    German army units reach Smolensk.

21st August 1941    The first Arctic convoy carrying aid to Russia sails to Archangel.

| | |
|---|---|
| 15th September 1941 | Leningrad is cut off and besieged. |
| 30th October 1941 | Severe snow halts the German advance in the east. |
| 7th December 1941 | Japanese carrier-based aircraft launch a surprise attack on Pearl Harbour in Hawaii. Five American battleships are sunk along with a number of cruisers and destroyers but the aircraft carriers are out at sea and thus survive the raid. |
| 8th December 1941 | Britain, along with the USA, declares war on Japan. |
| 9th December 1941 | Japanese forces land in Malaysia and Thailand. |
| 10th December 1941 | HMS *Prince of Wales* and *Repulse* are sunk by Japanese bombers off the coast of Malaysia. |
| 11th December 1941 | Germany declares war on America. |
| 25th December 1941 | Hong Kong falls to the Japanese. |
| 15th January 1942 | Japanese troops invade Burma. |
| 15th February 1941 | Singapore surrenders to the Japanese. Over 100,000 British and Commonwealth troops are taken prisoner. |
| 16th April 1942 | The island of Malta, which has stoutly resisted air attack by Italian and German forces, is awarded the George Medal by the King. |
| 39th May 1942 | British Bomber Command launches the first Thousand Bomber raid on the city of Cologne in Germany. |
| 6th June 1942 | The Battle of Midway – the Japanese lose four aircraft carriers in their first setback of the war. |
| 21st June 1942 | Germany's *Afrika Korps* finally take Tobruk – Rommel is promoted to Field Marshal. He pushes on with his advance, crossing the border into Egypt. |
| 7th August 1942 | Montgomery is appointed to lead the British Eighth Army in Africa when General Gott is killed in an air crash. |
| 19th August 1942 | The Dieppe raid, involving 5,000 allied soldiers in an assault on the French coast, is a disaster, over half the force becoming casualties. |

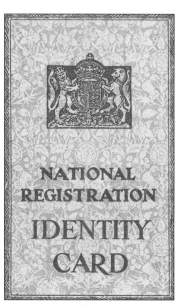

NATIONAL REGISTRATION IDENTITY CARD

All British subjects were issued with Identity Cards during the war.

| | |
|---|---|
| 31st August 1942 | The German army in Russia approaches Stalingrad – by the following day they are engaged in hand-to-hand fighting in the suburbs of the city. |
| 7th September 1942 | Montgomery stops Rommel's advance at the Battle of Alam Halfa. |
| 8th September 1942 | US Marines land on Guadalcanal. |
| 24th October 1942 | The Battle of El Alamein sees Montgomery halt Rommel's advance and then push forward the British line. |
| 8th November 1942 | Operation Torch – American troops in North Africa launch their first offensive in the European theatre of war. |
| 14th January 1943 | The Casablanca Conference begins – Churchill and Roosevelt discuss strategy for Britain and America for the rest of the war. |
| 31st January 1943 | Field Marshal Paulus surrenders in Stalingrad. Some forces under General Stecker continue to fight for a further two days before they, too, finally lay down their arms. Hitler is furious but orders a three-day period of national mourning. |
| 4th February 1943 | Montgomery's Eighth Army moves into Tunisia. |
| 5th March 1943 | The RAF begins bombing raids on the Ruhr industrial area in Germany. |
| 9th July 1943 | Allied forces land in Sicily. Clever deception has convinced the Germans that the landings will be in Sardinia. By 22nd July, Palermo has fallen to General Patton. |
| 25th July 1943 | Mussolini is relieved of his office as Italian leader and arrested. |
| 3rd September 1943 | Montgomery's Eighth Army lands in mainland Italy. |
| 8th September 1943 | The Italians surrender and the following day allied forces land at Salerno. They are met by fierce resistance from German troops. |
| 14th November 1943 | The Battle of Monte Casino begins. |
| 18th November 1943 | Over 400 RAF bombers raid Berlin. |
| 26th December 1943 | The *Scharnhorst* is sunk by HMS *Duke of York*. |
| 22nd January 1944 | The allies land at Anzio – after little initial resistance the troops are soon involved in bitter fighting with German units. |
| 10th April 1944 | Russian troops retake Odessa in the Crimea. |
| 18th May 1944 | Field Marshal von Rundstedt is appointed Commander in Chief (West), ready for the allied invasion of Europe. |
| 4th June 1944 | US forces enter Rome on the same day that the invasion barges from Britain sail for France – unfortunately they are recalled due to bad weather. |

| | |
|---|---|
| 6th June 1944 | The D-Day Landings (Operation Overlord) take allied troops back into mainland Europe for the first time in four years. Despite fierce resistance on Omaha Beach, by nightfall the bridgehead has been established. |
| 23rd June 1944 | Marshal Zhukov begins the Russian summer offensive. |
| 9th July 1944 | In the Pacific US Marines liberate Saipan while, in Europe, allied forces take Caen in northern France. |
| 17th July 1944 | Rommel is wounded after his car is attacked by allied aircraft. Later implicated in the bomb plot against Hitler, he takes his own life rather than face trial and see his family disgraced. |
| 20th July 1944 | The July Plot fails to eliminate Hitler when Count von Stauffenberg's bomb destroys the Wolf's Lair headquarters but leaves the Führer alive – and vowing vengeance. |
| 25th August 1944 | Paris is liberated. The following day General de Gaulle enters the city in triumph. |
| 8th September 1944 | The first V2 rocket – Hitler's new secret weapon – falls on London. Unlike the V1, this terror weapon makes no noise and takes just a few minutes to reach its target. |
| 17th September 1944 | The disastrous Arnhem assault (Operation Market Garden) is launched. Before the operation is over, 1000 paratroopers will have been killed and more than 5000 taken prisoner. |
| 6th November 1944 | Despite failing health, Roosevelt is elected for a fourth term of office as President of the U.S.A. |
| 16th December 1944 | In a last, desperate gamble the Germans launch the Battle of the Bulge against hard-pressed American troops in the Ardennes. It is nearly two weeks before the Americans regain the territory they have lost. |
| 17th January 1945 | The Russian army takes Warsaw. |
| 6th February 1945 | The Yalta Conference begins. Churchill, Stalin and Roosevelt meet to discuss the fate of the world after the war. |
| 19th February 19454 | US Marines land on Iwo Jima. |
| 7th March 1945 | Allied forces cross the Rhine by the Ludendorff Bridge at Remagen. |
| 20th March 1945 | Mandalay is captured from the Japanese by the 19th Indian Division. |
| 12th April 1945 | President Roosevelt dies. He is succeeded by Vice President Harry Truman. |
| 13th April 1945 | Allied troops enter Belsen and Buchenwald concentration camps –the full horror of the Nazi extermination process is revealed. |

| | |
|---|---|
| 25th April 1945 | American and Russian troops join up on the Elbe. |
| 28th April 1945 | Fleeing to Switzerland, Mussolini and his mistress are captured by partisans, shot and hung up by their heels on a patrol station near Lake Como. |
| 30th April 1945 | With Berlin surrounded, Hitler and Eva Braun, his wife of just a few hours, commit suicide in their bunker in Berlin. Joseph Goebbels survives him by only one day and Admiral Dönitz becomes Fürher. |
| 4th May 1945 | Germany surrenders at Luneberg Heath. |
| 8th May 1945 | VE Day is celebrated all over Europe. |
| 26th July 1945 | In British Parliamentary elections, Clement Atlee succeeds Churchill as Prime Minister. |
| 6th August 1945 | The first atomic bomb is dropped on the city of Hiroshima in Japan. |
| 9th August 1945 | A second atomic bomb hits the Japanese city of Nagasaki. |
| 13th August 1945 | Japan surrenders – VJ Day is celebrated. The war is finally over. |

Six years of war saw moments of triumph and disaster, glory and ignominy, for the people of Wales. Whether they spent the years between 1939 and 1945 in the forces or in factories, in their homes or in strange surroundings, ordinary people would have been aware of the war's progress. Newspaper reportage, a wireless in almost all homes, and newsreels in cinemas ensured that much of the reality – though shaped and possibly distorted in the telling – reached servicemen and women and civilians alike. It was a period that none of the people of Wales would ever forget.

'In the event of threatened air raids, warnings will be given in urban areas by means of sirens or hooters, which will be sounded in some places by short intermittent blasts and in other places by a warbling note changed every few seconds. The warnings may also be given by short blasts on police whistles. No hooter or siren may be sounded except on the instructions of the police.'

*The Daily Telegraph,* 4th September, 1939

# Chapter Two

# The Royal Monmouthshire
# Royal Engineers

In the final weeks before war was declared, Welsh soldiers, like soldiers right across Britain, were urgently mobilizing, ready to play their part in the coming conflict. During the last days of August 1939, as the crisis in Europe deepened, Regular, Reservist and Territorial troops gathered together at their bases or in newly-erected tented camps and waited impatiently for the orders that would send them off to war.

On Sunday 3rd September, Neville Chamberlain delivered his fateful message to the nation. In sad, broken tones the Prime Minister announced that, for the second time in twenty years, Britain was at war with Germany.

Almost immediately, Welsh soldiers and thousands of young men from across the country set off for places as far away as India, Egypt and France. As sandbags were deposited around important public buildings, as children played and sang – 'Under the spreading chestnut tree, Neville Chamberlain said to me, 'If you want to get your gas masks free, join the bleedin' ARP' was a popular ditty in these first weeks of war – the British Expeditionary Force embarked for France.

Committed by treaty to send troops to aid the French, by the middle of October 1939 Britain had 158,000 soldiers serving in France and Belgium with the BEF under the command of Lord Gort, VC, and the number was growing. The Welsh contingent was significant. Amongst them were the men of the Royal Monmouthshire Royal Engineers militia regiment.

The Royal Monmouthshire Royal Engineers was (and is) one of the oldest regiments in the British army. It is unique in that it features the word 'Royal' twice in its title, one 'Royal' having been inherited from the Militia, the other being owed to the Royal Engineers. With a history dating back to the 1530s, the regiment drew its part-time soldiers from towns like Monmouth, Abergavenny and Newport and from the rural areas of south-east Wales.

The stories of three men from the RMRE – LEN JENKINS, CHARLIE STERRY and BERNARD GIBBON – stand as representative of the countless thousands of Welsh soldiers who served across the globe in a wide range of operational theatres and environments during the war; ordinary soldiers and men caught up in a vast machine of killing and death. Their stories are unique but in the dangers they faced and in the way that they faced them they are also universal.

When the BEF arrived in France they were met, initially, by what is now known as 'the phoney war', long months of inactivity when Hitler – and the allies – built up military strength and waited for the easier campaigning days of early spring. For

Within days of war being declared, the BEF had departed for France.

many of the part-time soldiers, there was time to enjoy the experience and to reflect on how they had come to be in France in the first place.

LEN JENKINS, 101 Company RMRE

> I was born and bred in Monmouth so I knew most of the boys from the RMRE. I used to go up to the depot and play cricket with them in the evenings. The adjutant said, why didn't I join, and in the end I did. It was 1938 I was sworn in, although I suppose I'd been with them, playing sport and going on camps, since 1936.

BERNARD GIBBON, 100 Company RMRE

> I volunteered for the Reserve in, I think, 1938. It was a friend's idea but I was happy to go along with it – well, you did in those days. We used to meet in a drill hall on Stow Hill, even though the regiment's real base was in Monmouth.

CHARLIE STERRY, 100 Company RMRE

> I joined the regiment way back in 1937. I don't know if we expected war but it was a bit of fun, doing all the camps and training and that. We'd actually just done our summer camp when war was declared in 1939. Our Company was made up of Newport boys mainly.

The build-up to war had been a long and protracted process but many people had seen it coming – ever since Hitler had climbed to power in Germany in 1933. Chamberlain's announcement on 3rd September, however, took many people by surprise – even though they had been following events in the newspapers for many weeks

CHARLIE STERRY

I was actually watching a football match, watching Newport County play Tottenham Hotspur on the Thursday afternoon – the Thursday before war was declared. We got called over the 'mike', all the RMRE boys, to report back to Monmouth immediately. Things were starting to happen.

LEN JENKINS

That Sunday war broke out we were in church and at 11 o'clock the vicar told us that war had been declared. We went back to camp and they issued us with our kit. We were there, I think, for about a fortnight before they sent us by road to Newport, to Tredegar Park. We stopped there for the night and on the Saturday evening we went to Newport docks. They put us on the *Ben McCree* and next day we were off.

BERNARD GIBBON

We hung about for a week or so at Monmouth before they sent us off. We all had special dress uniforms but they wanted us in our old clothes. So we had to go in the middle of the parade ground and change our trousers! We went to the docks at Newport and onto the Isle of Man steamer *Ben McCree* and she sailed on the Sunday morning. My father had come to see the troops off. He didn't even know that I was there, on board.

CHARLIE STERRY

We landed at Nantes and sat around for a couple of days. We were given a pound when we went ashore and I'm pretty sure we got lots of francs when we changed our money. Anyway, we all had a pound. I remember going into this café and there was a one-armed bandit. I put 10 centimes in, pulled the handle and walked away. As I walked away the jackpot fell and, of course, you had to spend the money in the café. So the boys all had free drinks till it was gone.

Charlie Sterry (right) and a fellow soldier in France in 1939.

BERNARD GIBBON

> I was a motor mechanic and driver. We had old six-wheeled vehicles with the four driving wheels at the back. CDFs they were called. They were all fixed up so you could only do about 30 miles an hour. But after a bit we got those governors fixed. We shortened the string on the butterfly of the carburettors and soon those old trucks were flying along at 60 miles an hour.

LEN JENKINS

> We went up into northern France, to Vimy Ridge outside Lens, by the old First World War battlefield. We were there for about three months, clearing up the woods and finding lots of ammunition from the First World War. We made an ammo dump for the artillery following us up.

The Royal Monmouthshire Royal Engineer units in France at this time consisted of men from 100 and 101 Companies. They were attached to the headquarters of the BEF, 100 Company constructing buildings and roads, 101 Company supporting the forward HQ of Lord Gort. Consequently, they were often asked to carry out interesting and unusual tasks, many of them a far cry from the traditional jobs associated with soldiers in the front line.

LEN JENKINS

> Once I was picked to go with Lt Cooper and Driver Adams to Paris to find a bath with a heating apparatus for King George VI. He was coming over to visit us at the end of 1939, just before Christmas. We found the bath and took it back to the chateau at Arblack, about ten miles from Beaumetz. One of our plumbers, a chap called Carter, was actually under the bath connecting up the pipes when the king walked in. The king spoke to him and even gave him a Christmas box.

Len Jenkins (left) at an *estaminet* on Vimy Ridge in 1939. Also in the photograph are (L to R) a French soldier, the *estaminet* owner and Sapper Jones. The girl in front of the group is the daughter of the *estaminet* owner.

It was not all work, however. Sometimes there was light relief from the monotony of waiting, as the soldiers called it, 'for the balloon to go up'.

BERNARD GIBBON

> We were working in conjunction with the French army in those days. Every morning I'd drive our French interpreter around on reconnaissance. We could see the Germans over their lines. The interpreter used to say, 'Gibbon has his rifle, I have my revolver. We're quite safe. Don't worry, Gibbon, only one bullet in thirty ever hits its target.'

LEN JENKINS

> In our spare time we used to go to an *estaminet* or to the Naffi and play darts and skittles. Once a month, or perhaps every six weeks, we had ENSA come over to entertain us. We had Gracie Fields once, then Harvey, the comedian, and several more. Another time we were sent George Carpentier, the boxer. He came and we had a couple of boys from Newport who boxed. He mixed it with them, three rounds apiece.

CHARLIE STERRY

> I was a transport driver and in those days I spent my time driving supplies around. It was a good time. We had a beautiful billet – I'd like that billet all over again. The people around us were really nice, they made you welcome. They even invited you out for Sunday dinner.

When the German attack began on 10th May, 1940, it was sudden and decisive. The German army swept into the Netherlands, Belgium and Luxembourg, faced by little or no opposition and resistance. By 15th May the Dutch had stopped fighting – the day before, it had been the turn of the French to face assault.

The Maginot Line, the supposedly indestructible and impenetrable series of forts and defensive works between France and Germany, had been meant for just such an eventuality. The line was incomplete, however, and there were serious gaps in the fortifications. Hitler's Blitzkreig (or 'lightning war') simply tore through or by-passed the Maginot Line. Tanks and infantry, supported by wave after wave of dive bombers, raced for the Channel and for Paris, leaving behind battered, defeated and dead allied soldiers.

The BEF found itself trapped in a pocket between thousands of victorious German soldiers. Cut off and isolated, Lord Gort had no option but to order a withdrawal towards the coast between Zeebrugge and Boulogne. For the first time, people in Britain heard about the beaches of Dunkirk, where their soldiers were now stranded. The suddenness of the attack had caught everyone by surprise.

CHARLIE STERRY

> The French were going up with horse-drawn guns and the Stukkas came over and bombed. We missed it – the French caught it. Me, like a silly bloody fool, I jumped down and went under the wagon. I'd have been blown to pieces if they'd hit us – there was explosives in that wagon. I wasn't thinking, just diving for cover. Anyway, the French artillery caught the lot.

LEN JENKINS

When the attack came in May we were sent out as infantry – anything to try and stop their advance. We were at Beaumetz when the planes came over, bombing. They were so low, as low as the ceiling. Whenever we moved the planes would run along the road and open up with their machine guns. We'd dive into a ditch, no matter where it was, just trying to save ourselves. The road was full of refugees with ponies and lorries and pushchairs and everything packed together like a Bank Holiday at the seaside. Oh, it was a pity to see them all.

BERNARD GIBBON

Our headquarters was down the hill, at the back of Mont Cassell. My officer, Lt Whittaker, told me to go down and get rations. We had two dixies, full of stew, when we were driving back up the hill. We were being shelled at the time and one of the wheels at the back of the wagon got damaged. I climbed out to see what I could do. The tyre was blown off and the wheel was bent around the brake drum. Whittaker was sat in the front of the wagon and these two other guys, Sappers Winston and Tamplin, were in the back. I managed to lever off the damaged wheel and replace it. I was cursing at the others for not giving me a hand but when I went to give them hell I found that Tamplin had been wounded by a shell splinter. It had gone right through his helmet into his head – he'd been wearing an old French helmet. Winston was too shocked to do anything.

I dropped the two of them at the aid station. They were on the move and didn't want to take them at first. They did in the end.

As we went up the hill, down came the Colonel's car. We stopped to ask for instructions and the Colonel poked his head out of the window and said, 'Make your own way back, make your own way back.' Well, it didn't make sense to us, so I returned to Company HQ. I parked the vehicle in the field and Sergeant Smith told me we'd had orders to abandon all vehicles and walk to Dunkirk.

Bernard Gibbon, RMRE.

LEN JENKINS

> We were on Mont Cassell when, at ten in the morning, they said, 'Make your own way to Dunkirk.' We all jumped into the tank trap and ran along that for about an hour. Then over came another plane and started machine-gunning. My mates all ran into a house that was close by but I thought, 'If he bombs that, we've got no hope at all.' So I ran the other way and got into a ditch. I didn't see my mates again.

CHARLIE STERRY

> We took up positions on bridges over a canal. All the refugees were going through and we were waiting to blow the bridges in the area. Eventually we blew them and congregated back in a field, the whole Company, right around the edge. The cars were camouflaged, all the way round the field. From there we went up onto Mont Cassell. I'd really like to know why we went to Mont Cassell while 1 and 3 Sections moved off to Dunkirk.

Charlie Sterry (2nd from left, front row) with fellow soldiers in France.

BERNARD GIBBON

> It wasn't just bridges we had to destroy. Once, they told us to blow up this oil refinery. So we went and destroyed the tanks – imagine the flames and the smoke? They all went up except one. It just didn't go. And then, when there was only the one left, the order came through *not* to destroy them.

CHARLIE STERRY

We were on Mont Cassell for about three or four days. The Jerries did try to come up with tanks but there was no way through. And then, in the early hours, they led us out, single file, and marched us up the road, Captain Deacon in front with the French interpreter. We had the Welsh Guards with us, the Gloucesters and lots of other regiments. We were supposed to be making for Dunkirk but it was too late of course, the Jerries were waiting. We got so far and they ambushed us. They had everything there and they just opened up.

Captain Deacon was the first one to catch it, across the cheeks of his bottom. Everybody dived into a ditch. Then a bren-gun carrier came sailing up the road, swung round and came straight back down. The Jerries didn't fire on it because they knew we weren't going anywhere. They wanted it intact. We were trapped.

A British anti-tank gun in action – it didn't stop the German Panzers.

LEN JENKINS

I came to a canal and this chap said, 'There's a bridge down there but you'd better be quick, we're going to blow it in a quarter of an hour.' So I ran down and joined up with a group of Welsh Guards. I stopped with them a bit because I thought we were all going to Dunkirk. Then they said they weren't headed for Dunkirk, they were going back into action. So I got out.

When I came into Dunkirk all the Frenchmen were singing and dancing at this *estaminet* as I passed. 'What's on?' I asked them. They just said they were enjoying themselves. They probably were, they were drinking that much! I thought the war must be over. I went on down to the beach and met one or two of my mates there.

### BERNARD GIBBON

When the order came to abandon our vehicles I wasn't going to leave mine. Earlier on I'd passed a Wine and Spirits Store in Douai. There was nobody there so we filled up the vehicle with bottles and things. I'd already collected 25,000 Goldflake from a Naffi somewhere.

I said to the Transport Sergeant, Smith his name was, 'Look, Smithie, I'm getting my bloody truck out from here. I'm not leaving 25,000 Goldflakes in it.' Smithie said, 'If you get yours out, we all will.' By now we were being shelled heavily so we moved out and joined a convoy on the road.

The retreat to Dunkirk was a chaotic affair – 'organised chaos' as Bernard Gibbon called it. 'Make your own way back' seems to have been the order of the day. Men from 100 and 101 Companies of the RMRE had undertaken valuable work in the retreat, blowing up fuel stores and bridges in an attempt to slow the German advance. It was exhausting and dangerous work.

Eventually, most of 100 Company were captured and spent the rest of the war as POWs. The men of 101 Company were, in the main, luckier and after many anxious moments were able to reach the Dunkirk beaches.

### CHARLIE STERRY

I ended up in a field. I don't know how I got there but I found myself in this field. I was on my 'Jack Jones' by now, trying to get under some barbed wire. I couldn't because of the valise on my back. So I took it off and crawled under. I finished up at the back of this house and all of a sudden there was a whine and I caught it in the leg.

### BERNARD GIBBON

We were at the tail end of the convoy and as I was driving I looked across the field and there were these blokes in grey uniforms coming towards us, a long line of them. 'Germans!' I said to Lt Whittaker, 'bloody Germans, sir.' He looked and said, 'Good God, Gibbon, get moving.' So I just swung the wheel and went through the other hedge and was away.

Bernard Gibbon (sitting, right) and colleagues in the early years of the war.

CHARLIE STERRY

>After I was hit I scrambled along for a bit and eventually fell into a dug-out. Who should be there but our French interpreter – he was hiding in there. He took all my emergency bandages and used them to stop the bleeding in my leg.

>All of a sudden it went quiet. You could hear a pin drop. Then out of the house came this great big Jerry, smoking a cigar. I said to the interpreter, 'I could pot him.' But he said, 'No, don't do that.'

>Then I heard our boys shouting, 'Tops, Tops?' They used to call me Tops. The interpreter said, 'Say nothing.' But I couldn't resist it in the end so I shouted, 'Here I am.'

>They came and carried me out on a door to the German casualty station where I was seen to. The boys left me a couple of cans, supposed to be full of water. In fact they were full of cognac. That was it. I got captured when I called, 'Here I am.'

BERNARD GIBBON

>We were stopped several times by MPs telling us to park the vehicle and walk to Dunkirk. We had a GHQ sign on the front of the truck – 42, I think it was, with a white bar. Well, Lt Whittaker was wearing his white mac, without rank or insignia, and he kept getting out and saying, 'Don't you know who we are?' and pointing at the GHQ sign. So they just waved us through and in the end we drove right onto Bray Dunes at Dunkirk.

The rescue of the BEF, along with hundreds of French and Belgian troops, from the beaches of Dunkirk is one of the most remarkable stories of the war. Orders to begin the evacuation were given on 20th May and from the coasts, rivers and creeks of southern England a huge armada of 'little ships' – over 800 of them – set off across the Channel to rescue the trapped army.

Ships of the Royal and Merchant Navies stood off-shore while the launches and pleasure boats ferried exhausted soldiers to the safety of the larger vessels. By 4th June, when the destroyer HMS *Shikari* left Dunkirk with the last of the troops on board, over 200,000 British and 112,000 French soldiers had been saved. It was a remarkable achievement but, despite the efforts of Britain's new Prime Minister Winston Churchill to turn the exercise into glorious victory, this was still a defeat of major proportions.

Despite the enormous number of men rescued, 68,111 soldiers from the BEF had been killed, wounded or taken prisoner. A total of 243 ships had been lost and 2,472 guns, 63,879 vehicles and 76,000 tons of ammunition had been left behind on the beaches. And there were times that the miracle of the evacuation and the little ships seemed to be more by accident than by design.

LEN JENKINS

>We didn't know what would be waiting for us at Dunkirk, whether there'd be boats or whatever. When we got there we found nothing. A lot of men had been out in the water and been drowned or killed by the planes. They'd been

washed back in and they were lying on the beach, at the water's edge. And kit? Oh, the beach was full of it.

Once on the beach, soldiers were left to their own devices. They lay in the dunes or stood patiently in long lines across the sand, many of them up to their necks in water. The little ships pulled in to the beach, destroyers and peace-time pleasure steamers tied up alongside the mole. Soldiers everywhere wondered if they were ever going to get away.

LEN JENKINS

I saw this boat about twenty yards out and I said to my mates, 'Come on, let's see if we can get on there.' We walked into the water, up to our waists we were, and climbed onto the boat. Then this officer came along and asked what Division we were in. I told him GHQ. 'Get off!' he shouted. 'You don't belong to us.' So we had to get off the boat and wade back to the beach.

BERNARD GIBBON

Having parked up on the beach we went scrounging. I found myself a little Austin 7 Tourer and we used this to ferry people up and down the beach and to the boats. We found an old Thornycroft army launch, beyond the water level, and I was able to get the motor going. But that night an artillery Major came along, saying, 'I have been given command of this boat.' He said he had to get back to London to see the Prime Minister. Later I was told it was Churchill's son, Randolph, but I don't know if that's true.

Anyway, the first thing this Major did was turn the boat sideways on to beach. I got the engine going again and he did the same thing again. Then he started swearing, saying there were too many of us on board. I jumped off, into 12 feet of water, and went storming back up the beach. I found Lt Whittaker, his batman and another officer and started swearing about this artillery Major and the stupidity of senior officers sending him down to the boat. Then Whittaker said, 'Gibbon, this is the Colonel.' I hadn't recognized him in the dark.

LEN JENKINS

We lay there on the beach, trying to dry off. Jerry came over in the morning and machine-gunned us for about an hour. He dropped everything he had on us.

CHARLIE STERRY

All of the units doing the rearguard action – the Gloucesters, the Durham Light Infantry, the Green Howards, the Welsh Guards – they all got captured. And us along with them.

The rearguard may have been sacrificed but at least they gained valuable time to enable the evacuation to take place. Many soldiers fell into enemy hands simply by taking the wrong turning during the hike back to the sea, walking down the wrong road and blundering into the advancing Germans. For the men on the beaches, however, there was still the chance of rescue and safety.

LEN JENKINS

> In the morning I looked up and, suddenly, there was a rowing boat coming towards us. It was just bouncing about on the waves and the oars were in the bottom of the boat. There was nobody on board, nobody at all. I expect somebody had taken it out to one of the destroyers and then just cast it off. Now it was floating back in on the tide.
>
> I said to my mates, 'Come on, I know you two can row.' And we ran down to the water. I thought, 'This is it – now or never.'
>
> Before we got very far there were, suddenly, about twenty blokes in the water alongside us, all trying to climb in. I said, 'Here, steady, the boat'll sink. We'll send it back for you.' So we kept pulling and pulling and all of a sudden a motor boat came past. The bloke threw a rope across and towed us out to the destroyer *Collingdale*.

BERNARD GIBBON

> We found an engineers' folding boat and we carried it around the corner of the beach, down to the HQ. We rowed out to this destroyer on the horizon, HMS *Windsor*. We climbed up the rope ladders on her side and she was full of English officers and French and Belgian troops. Lt Whittaker detailed some Belgians to take the boat back to the beach.

LEN JENKINS

> When we got on board the *Collingdale* we had to make a chain gang, handing up shells from the magazine to the guns. The sky was black with Jerries and we were working for about two hours. Jerry was bombing and machine-gunning us. We had no air force there – the only time I saw them was when we got back to Dover and there was the air force, up on the cliff, waving and shouting to us.

BERNARD GIBBON

> I had my pack full of bottles of whisky and Goldflake and some of the staff officers gathered round – a bit jealous of all I'd got. On the way across the Channel we passed some of the small boats and landed in Dover on a Thursday evening.

LEN JENKINS

> All of a sudden the *Windsor* just drifted off and we were away. We arrived in Dover on 2nd June, about eight at night. We handed in our rifles and ammunition and got onto the train. I had been issued with 50 rounds of ammunition at Monmouth in September 1939 and when I came back from Dunkirk I had the same fifty rounds and the same rifle. I'd never fired. But I tell you what, when I got to Dover I was as happy as all the birds in the air.

Arriving back in Britain was not the end of the affair for many soldiers. From Dover they had to find their way back to their bases or home areas. And there was always the thought that for many of their comrades there would never be a return home, ever.

BERNARD GIBBON

> Three hundred of us from 100 Company went out to France in 1939. Only a hundred came back. That's two hundred lost – all friends.

All that was left of 100 Company RMRE after the Dunkirk evacuation.

LEN JENKINS

> It had never dawned on me that I might die. I just thought, 'Do your best and keep going.' When I got back I thought to myself, 'Well, that's one lot you've got through. What's the next lot likely to be?'

BERNARD GIBBON

> Lt Whittaker stayed with us at Dover, booked us in at the railway station and got us ten bob each. Then he came with us till we reached Swindon. That was on the Friday morning.
>
> My mate Ken Jones and I managed to get a bath at a vicar's house and then we walked down the street into town. There was a house with a bay window, being used by some unit or other. The window was open so Ken and I looked in. There was a big pad of leave forms just lying there. We removed these and stopped an officer on the street and got him to sign them for us. Then we went home to Newport for weekend leave.

LEN JENKINS

> We travelled for hours to Aldershot and got there about twelve o'clock at night. They turned us around and sent us to Tidworth, to St Martha's Barracks.

Tidworth had little appeal for Len Jenkins. The place was empty, there was nothing to do and so he and one of his friends decided to hitch-hike home. After a number of different lifts they arrived in Tetbury.

LEN JENKINS

A gentleman came up to us and said, 'You two look rough. Where have you come from?' We said, 'Dunkirk.' 'Oh,' he said, 'come in and have some fish and chips and a cup of tea.' So we were in this café, nice and comfortable. He said, 'Now don't move from here and I'll fix you up.' He sent a Sergeant and two coppers in and they took us to the police station.

'I'm doing this for your own good,' he said. 'If I let you go along the road tonight you'll get shot. I'll look after you and put you right in the morning.' He put us in the cells and gave us a cup of coffee. In the morning his wife gave us bacon and eggs and ten shillings apiece. I was in Monmouth by half-past nine, maybe ten o'clock, in the morning.

For those who had been taken prisoner by the Germans, however, there would be no going home for several years. The bitterness of defeat was sometimes hard to bear.

CHARLIE STERRY

I was sent to a hospital in Cambrai, controlled by British officers. They plastered my leg from the foot up, then they transferred us for a while to Lille, to a monastery. I couldn't walk so I had to borrow somebody's stick to go to the toilet. I fell down and couldn't get up again. A Captain of the Welsh Guards picked me up and we had a little chat. He said, 'We've got a Tom Sterry in my Company.' I replied 'That's my brother.' He'd got away but the Captain and some of the others had been captured.

Once Charlie Sterry was fit and recovered from his wound, prisoner-of-war camp beckoned. Before long he was discharged from Lille and sent off to Camp Stalag VIIIB.

CHARLIE STERRY

They put us in cattle trucks and sent us off into Germany. When we stopped they marched us up from the station, past all the Swastikas and through the crowds of people. I don't know how to describe it, they were all cheering and shouting. Then they marched us to Stalag VIIIB.

The prisoner-of-war camp was on the Polish border and due to various stops en route, it had taken Charlie Sterry eight months to make the journey from his monastery to the camp. By obtaining and sewing on some Corporal's stripes he promptly made himself eligible for a working party outside the camp at a local brickworks.

CHARLIE STERRY

There was this lady, heavily pregnant, and she was carrying two pails of water from the pump that everyone had to use. I went over and got hold of the pails and carried them for her. Of course, the boys were taking the piss out of me, saying I was fraternizing, but I didn't take any notice. I thought 'She's a human being and I'm a human being.' And from that day onward I filled that lady's buckets – they had a big bath till the day I left. I didn't realise that the lady I helped would eventually become my mother-in-law.

Anyway, one day her daughter was passing our billet on her bike and, of course, I wolf-whistled. I got to know her and one thing led to another. We did our bit of courting and today she's my wife. Her name is Julia, she was Julia Muller. She was a Sudeten German. Although her birth certificate says she's Czech, she is actually from the Sudetenland.

As the war went on Charlie Sterry and his future wife continued their courtship, sometimes at great risk to all concerned.

CHARLIE STERRY

The Gestapo tried to put a stop to it. They were going to send me away somewhere – I'd already packed my bags. But I think the manager of the brickworks put a stop on it. I can't see any other way it could have been. At that time, in Germany, they would have paraded Julia, scraped her head and paraded her for collaborating. But they didn't and I think the manager squared it. We must have been valuable to him or something.

Valuable they may well have been, for Charlie Sterry and his comrades remained in Stalag VIIIB almost until the end of the war. In 1945 the Russians made a big push and as the Geneva Convention stated that any prisoners-of-war had to be at least thirty miles behind the front, the men had to be evacuated.

CHARLIE STERRY

They put us all on the march. As I was registered as being wounded they put me on a train and sent me to Prague. We eventually finished up in Nuremberg and got back to the Yank lines. When we arrived, there were these Salvation Army people lobbing out cups of coffee – and who should be there, giving out buns and coffee, but Marlene Dietrich. I even got her autograph.

They put us on Dakotas and flew us to Brussels. We were there, walking around the town like tramps for a couple of days, and then they put us into these Lancaster bombers. I was sitting in the middle turret and as we were flying home, the pilot said, 'We're going over Dunkirk now.' That's the nearest I came to Dunkirk, flying over the place!

Incredible experiences seem to have been part and parcel of the war for Charlie Sterry. And they were not finished yet. After arriving in Britain he and his comrades were de-loused, given a couple of pounds and new clothes and simply told to go home.

CHARLIE STERRY

I caught a train to Newport and there wasn't a soul on the station when I got there, apart from one person down the far end, waiting for a train. It was my sister waiting for her train to Marshfield.

And the lady who was to become his wife?

CHARLIE STERRY

I had to leave her behind. I went to the Czechoslovakian Embassy and gave them her details. She wrote and then, suddenly, out of the blue, she came over to Britain. An air force officer had befriended her. She never had his name or anything. I would have liked to have got in touch with that gentleman and thanked him.

Anyway, he paid her fare from Harwich. And he put her right for Paddington. She didn't have any money so she ended up at Paddington station and couldn't get any further. The police got in touch with me and asked if I would pay her fare to Newport. That's what I did and met her at the station.

It was so out of the blue. I was hoping we'd eventually get together but that was really out of the blue. She couldn't speak a word of English but we got married on Sunday, 21st March, 1948.

Charlie Sterry and his wife, Julia, taken not long after she followed him to Britain.

Charlie Sterry's story is an incredible tale of love, luck and determination. And for the other soldiers from the Royal Monmouthshire Royal Engineers whom I interviewed, the war also had an amazing effect on their lives. Their stories are full of humour, compassion and good fortune. Len Jenkins and Bernard Gibbon, like Charlie Sterry, faced their moments of danger and, in the end, won through.

Their wars did not end with the Dunkirk evacuation. Len and Bernard both went on to serve in other campaigns. For a while Bernard Gibbon was also involved in Civil Defence.

BERNARD GIBBON

> We had a spell in London, working with the fire brigade. We also helped out in
> Swansea during the Blitz – and Bath. It was really demolition and rescue
> work. It had to be done. It was war-time, wasn't it? I finished up in 615
> Squadron, Guards Armoured Division.

In 1944 Bernard Gibbon went back to France after the D-Day landings. A few
months later, he was seriously injured whilst clearing enemy mines and invalided
home.

Len Jenkins did not stay for long in Britain. Within a few months he was off on
his travels again.

LEN JENKINS

> I went out to the Middle East, to Egypt. We went on a New Zealand freighter
> as far as South Africa. Then at Durban we changed to the Dutch Blue Riband
> liner *Nieuw Amsterdam*. It was real luxury – there was even a swimming pool
> on board. We were on board her for about a fortnight, going up the Red Sea
> and into Egypt.

After that it was service with the famous Desert Rats and action in North Africa.
Following the invasion of Sicily and Italy he fought in the battle for Monte Casino
and, after many months of marching and campaigning in northern Italy, finished the
war in Austria – a far cry indeed from the sleepy streets of Monmouth.

> 'We shall go on to the end. We shall fight in France, we shall fight on the
> seas and oceans, we shall fight with growing confidence and growing
> strength in the air, we shall defend our island, whatever the cost may be, we
> shall fight on the beaches, we shall fight on the landing grounds, we shall
> fight in the fields and in the streets, we shall fight in the hills; we shall never
> surrender.'
>
> Winston Churchill, Speech to the House of Commons, 4th June, 1940

# Chapter Three

# The Home Front

Between 1940 and 1945, perhaps for the first time in history, the concept of 'total war' was brought home to the people of Great Britain in terrifying and shocking detail. The air raids which began in the autumn of 1940 – and returned with almost equal ferocity in the 'doodlebug' and V2 attacks of 1944 and 1945 – brought death and destruction on a scale that many people had never considered remotely possible.

Not since the Civil War of the 1640s had the civilian population of Britain been so intimately involved in conflict. There had been Zeppelin and Gotha bomber raids during the First World War and, on several occasions, German battle-cruisers had managed to shell Scarborough and other towns along the North Sea coast. Yet those experiences were nothing compared to the Blitz that Hitler unleashed on the country following the fall of France in 1940.

A few perceptive individuals had an inclination about what was to come. The Nazi destruction of Guernica during the Spanish Civil War had given an awful early indication of the value of aerial bombardment and there were those in positions of power who were prepared, privately at least, to voice concern.

Consequently, as early as May 1938, the British government issued instructions about what to do in the event of enemy air raids. Included in the information was advice about the warnings that would be given – the sirens, whistles and rattles that would be sounded – to alert the populace of impending air attack.

In July 1939, a few weeks before war, every house in Britain was sent a series of pamphlets on civil defence. At this late stage it had become obvious that civilians would be in the front line in the coming conflict, as much perhaps as soldiers serving in France or the Far East. In order to cope with the effects of war on the Home Front a large number of Civil Defence Workers would be required, everything from firemen and ARP Wardens to policemen, nurses and, eventually, the Home Guard.

When the bombing finally began it was terrifying. Streets and factories were razed to the ground; thousands of civilians lost their lives or were maimed and injured; everyone was shocked and startled by the ferocity of the experience.

Now, over half a century later, it is not easy to catch the essence of those dark days of 1940 and 1941. In some respects, trying to describe the strange combination of fear, regret and bloody-minded determination that gripped the country is like attempting to define the character of a nation at the most crucial period in its history. The Welsh poet Alun Lewis caught the incredible poignancy of the period when he wrote the following lines:

Softly the civilised
Centuries fall,
Paper on paper,
Peter on Paul.

Blue necklace left
On a charred chair
Tells that Beauty
Was startled there.

(from 'Raiders Dawn')

Perhaps most effective of all in conveying the reality of the attacks on the home front, however, are the memories of the Civil Defence Workers, men and women who, throughout the war years, simply turned up and did their jobs. Admired, ridiculed, praised, abused – Civil Defence Workers were the last line of defence in a bitter and cruel battle. Their war was unglamorous and brought few obvious rewards. Yet it was a battle that had to be fought. Without them it is highly likely that countless numbers of civilians would not have survived as they did.

People like firemen JOHN WALSH and HUBERT 'BUZZER' REYNOLDS and ARP runner JACK NEEDS were clearly aware of the job they had to do – and what it meant to them.

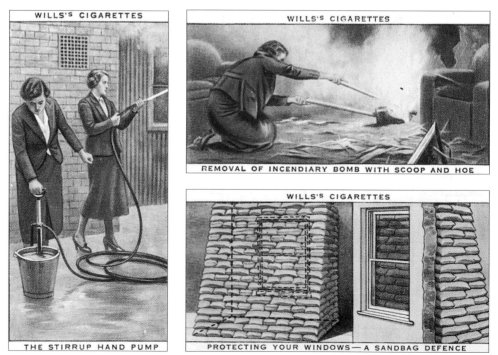

Cigarette cards like this WD and HO Wills 'Air Raid Precaution Set' were avidly collected by children during the war.

JOHN WALSH

I always felt I was doing some good for society in those war years – and afterwards as well, come to that. When we went to a fire, when we put it out and nobody lost their lives, when we rescued people, I used to think, 'We've done a good job.' I was always proud of being a fireman and of the job I did.

HUBERT 'BUZZER' REYNOLDS

As firemen you have to look after each other. You can't go it alone. You rely on your comrades and they rely on you, in the same way we relied on our armed forces, the RAF boys and the rest. We played our part. The boys in the armed forces gave their all – we gave all we could to help our people at home.

JACK NEEDS

My father was a First World War soldier. He'd lost an eye in that war. During the Second World War he was Senior Air Raid Warden in charge of a post. He used to organize everything. They had a rota which he'd work out. All the wardens, they took it very seriously. They knew what war was like.

In the battle against the German bombers, Air Raid Precaution Wardens were often at the sharp edge of the fight. Most of them, like Jack Needs' father, were old soldiers. They had seen butchery and brutality at first hand and were only too aware of the damage that could be done if people disobeyed orders. Failing to comply with blackout regulations was just one example of something to be avoided at all costs. In the early years of the war ESTELLE CLARKE was a young wife in Swansea, her husband serving away with the army. HARRY HIGHMAN was still a schoolboy in Newport. They both saw the power of ARP Wardens at first hand.

ESTELLE CLARKE

Well, you didn't dare switch a light on until you'd actually shut the door, till you'd checked that all your curtains were closed, were shut right across, and your windows black. Otherwise you'd get a very fierce shout from outside – 'Put out that light!'

HARRY HIGHMAN

There was always a warden patrolling. And if you showed a chink of light – the size of a matchbox – he'd be hammering at your door, saying, 'You're inviting a bomb to drop, you know.' How serious it was I don't know, to think you could see a chink of light from up there. But that's how it was then.

Sometimes the blackout caused as many problems as it solved, particularly when people found themselves in new or unusual places. MARY ROSE, or Mary Flynn as she was then, lived in the valleys beyond Cardiff and remembers the time and the problem only too well.

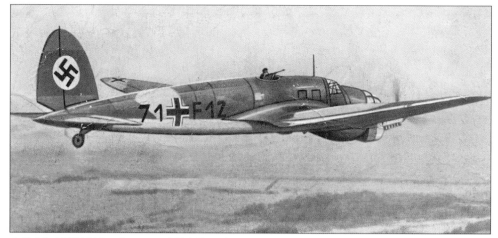

A Heinkel HE 111 bomber, one of Hitler's main weapons during the Battle of Britain.

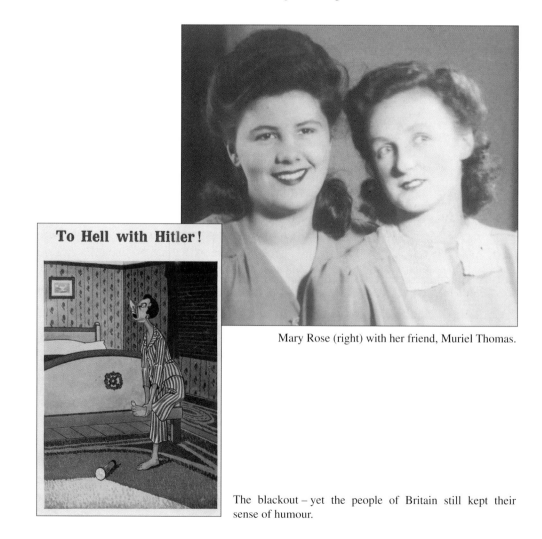

Mary Rose (right) with her friend, Muriel Thomas.

The blackout – yet the people of Britain still kept their sense of humour.

MARY ROSE

> I remember one incident about the blackout. I was courting at the time and my
> boyfriend and I went to Cardiff. We got on the wrong train and instead of going
> to Cardiff we ended up in Llanishen, which we didn't know anything about. We
> got out there and it was pitch black. We didn't know where we were.
>
> A gentleman came up behind us and said, 'Are you lost?' We said, 'Yes, we
> want to get to the platform to catch the train back.' He led us over the bridge
> and then we saw he was blind. We didn't know he was blind until he'd taken
> us over to the right platform. Well, of course, he was used to it. We weren't.

JACK NEEDS

> There were always arguments and fights about lights. Whatever you said,
> people always left lights on during the blackout. There was a fish shop in Clare
> Road, he always used to show a chink of light. 'Hey, what's that light?' we'd
> be shouting. Oh, they were very keen on not showing any lights like that.
> Whether it made any difference, I don't know.

MARY ROSE

> You would walk at night and you could hear footsteps behind you in the dark.
> But you couldn't see who it was. It was frightening, to walk like that in the
> dark.

In big towns like Swansea and Cardiff, the need to maintain a total blackout was
paramount, as DILYS OWEN and DORIS THOMAS can testify.

DILYS OWEN

> My father was an Air Raid Warden. As the war developed so all the younger
> men in the road had been called up. And he was about the youngest still there
> so he was the Air Raid Warden. Whenever there was a raid or when the air raid
> warning went he had to go outside straight away and walk the length of the
> road and right around it to make sure there were no lights showing – and that
> everybody was inside.

DORIS THOMAS

> I remember my father was an Air Raid Warden. When there was an alert on,
> every Air Raid Warden had a whistle and we used to open the side window of
> the house and stand there and blow the whistle. We all took it in turns, as
> children, to blow this whistle while my father was getting dressed to go out.

JACK NEEDS

> I was a messenger with the ARP wardens. I got trained exactly the same as
> them. We did the gas training, went into the gas cubicle and all that, just like
> the wardens. We also did a bit of first aid – some of the Wardens were really
> well trained in first aid, you know.

DILYS OWEN

One night there was a sound of planes, very low overhead. Much lower than we'd heard them before. And they dropped an awful lot – about a hundred, I think – of incendiary bombs and quite a lot of houses went on fire. My father was out for hours. And in fact we ran out, us children, ran out after him – which was a terrible thing to do because it left my mother in the house on her own. She was down in the cellar and she couldn't go out because she was very heavily pregnant.

JACK NEEDS

I became a runner for the ARP Wardens. After they'd trained me, I had a uniform and a bicycle. If the phones were out of action I was supposed to be one of the messenger boys, taking messages around to the other posts. But it never happened, thankfully.

I used to report to the Warden's post. My father was a Warden, then, and my mother. I used to patrol with them. I was only a young kid but, I tell you what, I was down by Grange Gardens one night when I heard this whistle and a thump. We had blocks on the road there, wooden blocks they used to be, covered with tar, for the trams. Anyway, I heard this thump. I went over and there was the nose cone off a shell embedded in the block. I dug it out and I've still got it, in the garage.

ELUNED GILES

Of course it was excitement for us children – all these people going about telling you what to do, blackouts on the windows. Having blackouts was great fun in the beginning. But it got to be a bit of a nuisance because they were so keen.

JACK NEEDS

The Wardens would have a rota. You'd go on duty at night, when it was your turn, and just patrol around. When a warning went, then we'd all turn out. It would be a Red Alert and our job would then be to try and rescue people, if we could.

Harry Highman lived directly opposite an ARP post in Newport. It was just one of many such posts and, to his delight, he was soon asked to become a messenger for the wardens.

WILLS'S CIGARETTES

AIR RAID PRECAUTIONS BADGE

HARRY HIGHMAN

> I was twelve years of age when the war started and I suppose, in some ways, I
> was self-appointed. I mean, the wardens were looking for people who lived
> near. Obviously they didn't want someone who was a quarter of a mile away.
> But I was within yards, really, of this post. I heard they wanted messengers.
> Then it was a case of 'Can I be one? Can I be one?' And so I got involved.
>
> There was usually only one person on duty in the post but in the event of a
> pending air raid – I forget the exact colour but I think it was an amber warning
> – all the other wardens would be called in. If they didn't have a telephone I
> would be asked to go and knock on their doors and say, 'Report for duty as
> soon as possible.'

The ARP post itself was not a purpose-built station. In the best tradition of 'make do
and mend' this was a conversion job and was only one of many such posts scattered
around towns like Newport. But for young boys like Harry Highman it was a place
of fascination.

HARRY HIGHMAN

> The ARP post was a garage underneath the house opposite. What they did,
> they put sandbags around the front of the doorway and at the side, sandbags
> probably about a foot wide and stacked up to ceiling height, outside the post
> itself.
>
> As children we were always playing at war. We didn't realize the horror of
> it. I can remember a friend's father saying to us, 'Before this war is over, you
> lads are going to be in it. It's going to be a long war.' And it was, six years of
> it.

As an ARP messenger or runner, the need for speed was vital. Having your own
bicycle was part of the deal.

HARRY HIGHMAN

> It was of one of the main factors, that you had your own bike. You didn't get
> any allowance for it, mind you. When the warning went you'd just get on your
> bike – or otherwise you ran. Most of the wardens lived within a quarter of a
> mile from the post so it was often easier to just run there, rather than ride.

Air raids brought death and destruction into the hearts of British cities. In an attempt
to protect the population, air-raid shelters were built in most towns. However, as
early as January 1939, the government had introduced small shelters that could be
placed in the back gardens of houses. Officially called sectional steel shelters, these
structures soon become known as Anderson Shelters, after the Home Secretary at
the time. BERNARD PARSONS, HARRY HIGHMAN and JACK NEEDS
remember their air-raid shelters in Cardiff and Newport.

BERNARD PARSONS

The government supplied these Anderson Shelters. They came up on a wagon and then the council workers decided where each one was going. And they dug this big hole to take it. They put the pieces of the shelter into the hole, then bolted it all together – both sides, then top and bottom with a big square for a door. There was another square at the other end, at the back of it, that you could undo as an emergency door.

Dad used to paint the inside of it, then throw sawdust on it because you used to get condensation inside. It used to be very wet and damp. In the end everything got damp. You'd go down there sometimes, after a heavy rain, and it could be flooded, 5 or 6 inches of water.

HARRY HIGHMAN

Most people put duckboards in their Anderson Shelter. We built bunk beds in ours and had a candle light as well. We made it warm because, with the Germans bombing Coventry or Bristol, quite often air-raid alerts would last for two, three, four hours.

The chappie next door, he was a keen distiller of rhubarb wine. He was an old soldier and if a raid was on for more than half an hour he'd say, 'I think we'd better have a little warmer.' And he'd bring out these little tots of wine. I knew I was under age but I used to look forward to having an air raid and hoping it would last more than half an hour.

A group of Civil Defence workers pose for the camera.

JACK NEEDS

We had a cellar which was an air-raid shelter; it was specially adapted. They concreted the floor and put corrugated sheets under the house, with pillars holding them. People used to come there every night. They all had their deck chairs and things in the cellar. And they'd bring in their dogs as well. I remember Mr and Mrs Dali from the fish shop in Corporation Road. They had a little Pekinese dog. They'd sit there in their deck chairs and you used to hear the dog snoring.

Towards the end of 1940 a new shelter was introduced for indoor use. This was the Morrison Shelter, a low steel cage named after the Minister for Home Defence, Herbert Morrison.

JACK NEEDS

Some people had wire-mesh shelters, like tables, and you could crawl under these in your living room. You didn't have to go outside. My mother used to prefer to go under the stairs. If anything happened, say thunder and lightning, it was grab the dog and get under the stairs. And it was the same when the warning went out during the war.

HARRY HIGHMAN

Morrison shelters – you have to appreciate that a lot of people didn't have any back gardens. They maybe lived in a flat. So a Morrison Shelter was, in effect, a steel table that you had in your dining room. It was a fairly thick steel plate, supported by angle-iron legs and a bit of mesh frame around it. So that if the house collapsed you'd be okay.

Most communities had their communal air raid shelters. These could be purpose-built or, more usually, were the converted basements of shops and cinemas. Sometimes, as in the case of London, underground stations were used. Often these public shelters were equipped with bunks and tables. The one factor that was common to them all was the sense of community that they helped to foster. In Cardiff PATTI FLYNN and ALAN WORRELL vividly remember the sense of companionship from those years.

PATTI FLYNN

What I remember most about the air raid shelters was the excitement of it all, being wrapped up in blankets at night, having a cup of cocoa – and my horror at the spiders in the corner. The community was absolutely marvellous. It was a time of rationing and shortage of food but everybody rallied round. I think, in times of trouble, people do rally together. This neighbourhood was, in particular, a very close neighbourhood. I'm talking about the Bay here and what they called the docks.

ALAN WORRELL

In Splott Park there was the usual swimming pool and games area with swings and slides. On this occasion we were crowded into the swimming pool and, believe me, they really used to jam them in. The air raid warning went but we didn't hear it. The pool attendant came around, shouting, 'Everybody out of the pool, out of the water.' So we got out, just as we were, in our bathing costumes, and went across the road into Baden Powell School which had air-raid shelters. And we spent the rest of the afternoon in those shelters, just sitting there with our bathers on!

Humour was important in those dark days. BARBARA NEWBERRY remembers one particular incident in the village of Gwespyr, close to the Point of Ayr collieries in North Wales.

BARBARA NEWBERRY

My father suggested that my mother and I go and stay with some friends in the village of Gwespyr – not far from Talacre – for a few days' rest.

One night there was heavy bombing on Liverpool and from the cottage windows, if you drew the curtains back just a wee bit, you could see all Liverpool and Birkenhead ablaze.

It was the after-effects of the Liverpool raid that she particularly remembers, however.

BARBARA NEWBERRY

One of the German bombers had three bombs left. He was getting out of the way so he did a circuit around North Wales and dropped these three bombs.
Number One bomb dropped just outside the village in an open field – no damage, just a crater in the ground.

Number Two bomb fell in a disused quarry – no problem there.

Number Three bomb – now that was a different story altogether. Number Three bomb dropped on the village bakery. And there was mayhem because next door, in the hall right next door to the bakery, that's where the colliery band stored their instruments and sheet music.

The village didn't want bread – they just wanted to save their instruments.

The town of Swansea suffered particularly badly from bombing raids during the first few years of war. The three-day blitz of 19th to 21st February 1941 reduced the town centre to rubble, crushing out life and wiping away buildings that had been landmarks for years. At the time MIRIAM EVANS was a seventeen-year-old girl in the town.

MIRIAM EVANS

We happened to be in chapel, in a Young Persons meeting, and then the siren went, the terrible wailing sound of the siren. Some people lived near enough and they went home. But we didn't live very near so we had to go into one of the rooms in the chapel to shelter. It was a very big building with many, many windows, too many windows to put up a blackout. Once the incendiary bombs started falling, these flares, they lit up the sky. There was a strange, eerie blue light everywhere.

ESTELLE CLARKE

It was the incendiary bombs that really worried you. It was more frightening to think that you could be burned to death, rather than blown up – which seemed quicker, somehow.

The blaze of burning Swansea could be seen for miles around, making it a great target for the enemy bombers – as GLESNI JONES recalls:

GLESNI JONES

We lived about thirty miles away from Swansea and if we went out through our back door we could see all of Swansea ablaze. The sky was dark red and I remember my parents telling me that bombs had been dropped on Swansea. And I wondered, what did they mean?

Fire-fighters at work in Swansea following the blitz.

MIRIAM EVANS

> You could hear the bombs whizzing down, making an awful noise as they came. And then a thud. As it happened, it was snowing and every time we had snow in Swansea, the Germans could pick out the river Tawe. Alongside that river there were different factories and works: steelworks, tin works, chemical works.
>
> We knew that there'd been many fires and we knew, obviously, houses had been destroyed. We didn't really know what was happening in the centre of town because we were a little way out. But even in our district there were fires. The bombs had just fallen everywhere. They were just trying to burn everything down.

ESTELLE CLARKE

> After the bombing people actually came down to have a look. And I found that horrific – to me that was ghoulish. I'd go the other way round rather than pass the bombed area. Perhaps that's, sort of, being blind to life as it was. I don't know.

The sense of tragedy was very real and for people like ELAINE PHILLIPS, who was just a child at the time, the raids on Swansea would change their lives forever.

ELAINE PHILLIPS

> My dad was working in a factory making munitions. He would say goodnight and off he would go. This particular night we were gathered in the kitchen where it was warm. It was a very cold night, I remember it was cold, but it was warm in the kitchen.
>
> The siren went and my grandmother said to my mother, 'It's very cold, shall we stay in?' And they pulled the table up against the windowsill. We went under the table and sat there. I could hear the droning noises and loud bangs. I was getting a bit fidgety and I said, 'Can I get my Sunny Stories book and my crayons?' I can remember my mother saying yes. I got my books and pencils and came back underneath the table. I was sitting there, scribbling away. And then there was a droning and a whistling noise. And everything went black.

With so many men serving away from home it was important to keep up public morale – good, old-fashioned sentiment was one way.

A Swansea street after the three-day blitz.                     *(Photo courtesy of West Glamorgan Archive Service)*

ESTELLE CLARKE

> We were always told that the one that killed you, you didn't hear. But they whistled as they went past – a very high-pitched whistle, really, depending on how close they were. Once they whistled – 'It's all right, it's gone over. Somebody else is going to be hit.'

ELAINE PHILLIPS

> I don't know how long I was unconscious but my first memory was that I woke up and I couldn't move. I couldn't move my head, I couldn't move my legs. I was pinned down. Everything was dark, there was pressure on me. And I suddenly realized that I had wet my knickers. And then I really cried because I was very upset about that.
>
> I reached out, feeling around, and I could feel – I knew it was my mother's hand. I was crying because I couldn't understand why she wasn't comforting me or speaking to me. And then everything went black again.

Elaine Phillips was just five years old when the war took away her mother and grandmother. As the raids increased in ferocity it soon became clear that nowhere in Britain was safe from the bombers. Cities, towns and villages all became targets for enemy aircraft.

Cwmparc, just outside Treorchy in the Rhondda, was subjected to a devastating raid on Tuesday, 29th April, 1941 when 27 people were killed. Six of them were children, two local boys and four evacuees.

Miner and Home Guard soldier HARRY RADCLIFFE, and MARY ROSE, who was a young girl in the area at the time, remember it well.

HARRY RADCLIFFE

> The biggest raid we had was on Treorchy. The whole street came down. I think it was a 'getaway', when a German aircraft was being chased. I went out to see the devastation afterwards. It was terrible, to see these coffins going down the street together. That's what really hit you. That's when you realised there was a war on.

MARY ROSE

> Two land mines and two bombs were dropped on Treharne Street in Cwmparc. My father was on duty because he was in the Council – they had a rescue team and he was on duty. We could see the flames from our back door and when Dad came home he was in a dreadful state because he'd helped to dig people out.
>
> Some were alive, some dead. It was very traumatic, it sort of brought the war close to us. Before it had been, sort of, far away.

For residents of Cwmparc the raid was a terrifying ordeal and when close relatives were lost it made the event even more real – as MARY EVANS, PEGGY MARS and VERA JAMESON remember.

## MARY EVANS

My father was out as an Air Raid Warden and he heard the bomb coming. So he ducked under the windowsill of next door. Of course when he stood up our house was flat. My father could hear my voice to guide him to where we were and he knew I was alive but he didn't know what was happening underneath.

If I could put my hand in a sitting position I could touch my mother's face and if I put my hand by my lap I could put it on the head of my aunt. My aunt died as they lifted her out and my mother was years getting over it.

## PEGGY MARS

The house was on top of us and we were screaming for help. We didn't hear a word from my mother or my sister. I think we must have had some sort of idea they had been killed because we couldn't hear a word from them.

We weren't dug out until morning. My arm was temporarily paralysed but in a way I was more fortunate than others. Nine of my family went that day. Nothing was ever the same again after that. Never.

## VERA JAMESON

We were evacuated from Manor Park in East Ham. I don't remember the explosion but when I came round I had a chair across my body – it saved me.

My legs were buried to my knees. I was buried for about ten hours before they got me out. I was just a ten-year-old child and when they started digging I could hear them talking – I thought it was Father Christmas coming down the trap in the ceiling.

My sister Joan, I saw her lying there and I knew she was dead. And my two brothers.

The Jameson family from Manor Park in London. Three died in the bombing of Cwmparc.
Back, left to right: George, Arthur.
Front, left to right: Vera (who survived), Joan.

PEGGY MARS

The two Jameson boys were brought out alive and they were taken to my aunt's house – they were using it as a first-aid post. The two boys got killed there when a land mine fell on it.

MARY ROSE.

The funeral was something nobody will forget, nobody who saw it. It was terrible. There were lorries, and all the coffins were lined up in the back of them. My dad didn't want to talk about it when he came in after the raid. He was grey. He said, 'Don't ask me any questions. I'll talk to you later.' He just wanted a hot bath and bed.

He did tell us afterwards. It was terrible, he said, digging people out. One woman was buried and she had a baby in her arms. They were both dead. Four of the dead were evacuees. That was ironic. They'd come down here to be safe and got killed.

For most people, however, it was simply a case of putting down their heads and carrying on as best they could. Churchill's speeches, his dramatic imagery and phrases about 'finest hours' and 'dying on the beaches', undoubtedly helped keep up the morale. Even so, for many people, children in particular, this was a terrifying time to be alive. Even in rural environments like Aberdyfi and Llansteffan, the fear was always there – as GAYNOR PUGH and EILUNED REES remember.

GAYNOR PUGH

Every night I'd look under the bed to see if Hitler was there. If he wasn't there I would get into bed and lie on my back. I didn't dare go onto one side or the other in case Hitler came from the back and stabbed me.

EILUNED REES

I was only three and a half when war broke out so I didn't really know any other way of life than wartime. I suppose the war didn't impinge on my life until my brother was shot down.

Death was something that was always present but people tried not to think about it, unless it was unavoidable. PATTI FLYNN has vivid memories of those days.

PATTI FLYNN

It must have been terrible for people like my mother. I was just a baby, not really aware of all the things that were going on. My father was a seaman, a sailor, and he died when I was about four years old. He was torpedoed at sea. My brother Joselyn had just gone missing – also at sea – a year before my father. And then my other brother, Arthur, he was in the RAF and his plane was shot down coming back from France about six months before the end of the war.

My mother remained a very strong person throughout. She gave us lots of love. I had two remaining sisters and a brother, and my mother kept the whole family together really well.

It was the sense of community, the feeling of all 'being in it together', that often helped pull people through. Support from neighbours and from family and friends was essential if people were going to survive in the weeks, months and years that followed.

'Road deaths in Great Britain have more than doubled since the introduction of the blackout, it was revealed by the Ministry of Transport accident figures for September. Last month 1130 people were killed, compared with 617 in August and 554 in September last year. Of these 633 were pedestrians.'

*The Daily Telegraph*, 31st October, 1941

# Chapter Four

# The Firemen

If there was one group of Civil Defence Workers who, more than any other, quickly grasped the seriousness of what they were facing, it was Britain's firemen. Once the Blitz began in the autumn of 1940 they were immediately involved in a terrifying nightly ordeal, trying to save lives and buildings.

In Wales things began slowly. Until the fall of France, most Welsh towns and ports were beyond the range of German aircraft. After the early summer of 1940, however, French airfields became available for the bombers and events began to gather pace. For four Welsh firemen, in particular – JOHN WALSH, HUBERT 'BUZZER' REYNOLDS, TED OWENS and WYNDHAM SCOURFIELD – it was to be a summer they would never forget.

JOHN WALSH

I was already in the Auxiliary Fire Service in Cardiff when war broke out. When the war clouds started gathering, they began getting volunteers into the AFS. Then, when war came, the AFS men became permanent firemen. I became a police fireman and lived in the docks police station. You have to understand that the National Fire Service wasn't in existence then.

HUBERT 'BUZZER' REYNOLDS

I was a police fireman when war broke out. I'd joined on 8th April, 1938, one of just five to be chosen from dozens who applied. I worked at the old Westgate Street Fire Station in Cardiff.

TED OWENS

I was only sixteen years old when the war began, living in Pembroke Dock. I went down, voluntarily, as a messenger boy with the local fire brigade. That was the old peace-time brigade, they hadn't even formed the AFS then. I met 'Pop' Morris, the fire chief at Pembroke Dock, and he was delighted to have me come into the station, running messages back and fore. I'd always wanted to join the fire brigade but to start with it was only voluntary. It was only after the big oil tank fire at Pembroke Dock that they took me on as a permanent, regular messenger boy.

WYNDHAM SCOURFIELD

I was living at Narberth in Pembrokeshire and working in Tenby as a plumber. When war broke out we were asked to join an organisation such as the Home

Guard or the fire service. The first fire engine in Narberth only came in December 1939 – before that all they had was a wooden cart, carrying pumps and buckets. Once they'd got a fire engine they asked for volunteer retained firemen. So I joined the AFS at about that time.

Once the Welsh towns came within the range of enemy bombers, the Cardiff firemen were quickly initiated into the art of fighting wartime fires.

JOHN WALSH

It was all really frightening and sad. I was at one fire in Queen Street. We had our turntable up and were fighting the fire. Then another couple of bombs dropped alongside us, in the same area, on and around the Carlton Hotel.

Years later, when I got married, we had our reception in the Carlton. Then later they pulled it down, and found an unexploded bomb there. My wife used to say that we must have been the only couple to have ever held their reception over an unexploded bomb.

HUBERT 'BUZZER' REYNOLDS

You didn't think of trauma in those days. There was no question of illness or depression. You just got on with it. Well, there was a war on in 1940. We'd go home now and again to see Mum and Dad but that was it. It was very hard when you think about it now.

For the rural brigades like Narberth it was all a bit of an adventure – at least in the early days of the war.

WYNDHAM SCOURFIELD

We had no experience of fires, none at all really, just some little chimney fires. All we had on the machine were ordinary nozzles for water, jets and stuff like that, not the equipment they've got today. I've often said that, at that time, all we had was a bit of brains, a bit of guts. That was all.

Things were about to get a lot harder. On Monday, 19th August, 1940 three Junker 88 bombers, escorted by a pair of Messerschmitt fighters, swept in over the south Pembrokeshire coast. Their target? The tank farm at Pembroke Dock.

Just one bomb hit the tanks but it was enough to start a devastating blaze that quickly grew to become the largest fire seen in Britain since the Great Fire of London, nearly three hundred years before.

During the three weeks that the fire raged, hundreds of men from 22 different brigades came to help, some from places as far away as Bristol and Birmingham. Thirty-eight firemen were seriously injured, many more received burns and minor injuries and, tragically, five men from Cardiff were killed when oil from one of the ruptured tanks engulfed them before they could escape. John Walsh and 'Buzzer' Reynolds were two of the Cardiff men sent to Pembroke Dock to lend assistance.

HUBERT 'BUZZER' REYNOLDS

I was on duty in Westgate Street with the morning watch and Inspector King and Superintendent Bainbridge, who were in charge, lined us up and said, 'You, you and you – you're going to Pembroke to fight a fire there. As you are, with your fire kit.' They brought a coach from the old South Wales Commercial Motors and off we went, not knowing what to expect.

JOHN WALSH

I was on standby in the docks police station in Mariah Street when I was ordered back to the docks. When I got back I was told, 'Get your fire kit and go up to the police station in Westgate Street.' When I got there, just in my fire kit – no change of clothes or anything – a crowd of other boys were there, some of them AFS, some regular firemen. We asked what was going on. They said, 'Oh, we can't tell you, it's secret. There's a coach coming in a minute. It's going to take you somewhere.' And away we went, with no idea where we were going.

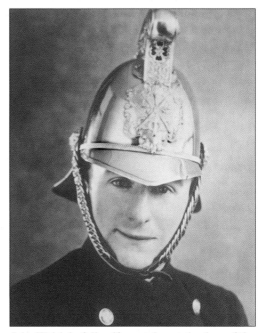

John Walsh in full uniform, taken at the time of the Pembroke Dock fire.

HUBERT 'BUZZER' REYNOLDS

I think we'd got as far as St Clears when we noticed the cloud. We didn't realize what was going on until we got a bit further and by then, of course, we were right in the middle of it.

JOHN WALSH

One of our boys said, 'Hey, look at that.' When we looked out there was a great big pall of smoke in the air, going over. We said, 'That's not the fire we're going to, is it?' Of course it was. The whole tank farm was on fire.

For the local men, almost from the beginning, they could see and understand the seriousness of the situation. Many of them had followed the path of the enemy bombers as they swept across the town. People like Ted Owens had even watched the bombs fall.

TED OWENS

I was at home at the time, in the garden. My grandfather kept a pub in Pembroke Street, an old-fashioned type of bar with wooden seats and clay pipes on the counter. Anyway, I was in the garden when the tanks were bombed.

I shouted to my mam, 'Look at that plane.' You could see the bombs dropping – no sound but you could see them. Of course, once they got up momentum you could hear them then. When the bang came I ran through the house to the front door because that was the direction it came from.

I could see this big pall of smoke going up. I didn't realize then that this column of smoke was the fire. I thought it was just the dust and debris.

WYNDHAM SCOURFIELD

There was a telephone call. They said they needed reinforcements for the Pembroke Dock fire. So we went down in cars, ordinary cars which had been taken over by the fire service. When I think of it now I think maybe I should have turned right round and gone the wrong way, gone back home. But as a youngster you don't see it, do you? When we approached the area the smoke was so intense you couldn't see where you were going.

TED OWENS

I'd stayed at the station when 'Pop' Morris and the boys had gone off to the fire. Then I had to run up to the tanks with a message. While I was up there they told me to go back to the station and send for as many brigades as possible – 'Pop' Morris knew they were going to need help.

When the bomb exploded on the oil tanks Pembroke Dock's fire brigade had gone straight to the scene of action. Fire chief Arthur Morris was the only full-time fireman in the station. The other members of the brigade were part-timers, volunteer firemen who were excited and keen to do what they could.

It hadn't taken the fire chief long to realize that the blaze was beyond the resources of his small brigade. More worrying, however, was the thought that if the fire at the oil tanks got out of control, then the whole of Llanreath and Pennar, small suburbs to the town of Pembroke Dock, could be incarcerated in a matter of moments. And so the call went out for help.

HUBERT 'BUZZER' REYNOLDS

How can you describe it? Nineteen oil tanks – frightening, absolutely frightening. We'd seen chimney fires and small fires in Cardiff but I just can't describe what we found there. It was tremendous – and the fact that Jerry was still coming over, underneath the smoke, using his machine guns.

JOHN WALSH

It was a sight I'll never forget. Oh, the flames, they were thirty or forty feet up in the sky and you wouldn't believe the width of them. You take an oil tank – well, there were flames that size going up into the air. And then the smoke. And oil dropping down. It was really frightening. You couldn't go too close because it was so hot. What we were doing was cooling the unaffected tanks and the ones on fire. But as one tank seemed to empty another would catch fire. That's how it went on.

HUBERT 'BUZZER' REYNOLDS

It was just like a dark cloud, oil-laden, and these fireballs in its midst, wrapped around the smoke. The heat – well, you felt that immediately. We only had our tunics, no protective clothing. And they were ruined.

The heat, you could feel it in the air – I suppose in the same way you feel it on a particularly hot summer day.

It just went on and on for three weeks. I'd be wrong to say I wasn't afraid – I'm not ashamed to say I was.

Hubert 'Buzzer' Reynolds.

A Junkers 88 bomber, the type of plane that attacked the oil tanks at Pembroke Dock.

WYNDHAM SCOURFIELD

Oh, the conditions were absolutely appalling. After half an hour you couldn't tell who was by your side. You were just covered in oil and smut. Some of the Pembroke Dock women were handing out towels. We ended up with towels on our heads and helmets, ordinary steel helmets, on top of the towels. So when the oil came off the helmet it would run down the towel and be hanging round your back.

All we had at that time were wellington boots and when you bent down all this oil and stuff went down your back, into your leggings, into your trousers, into your boots. That's why we had so much trouble with our feet. And your nostrils – you were blowing your nose and black oil was coming out. It was in your mouth, everywhere.

TED OWENS

After the second day people were getting hungry and thirsty because there was nothing up there, no canteen, nothing. So I went across to Llanreath, down into the orchards. I admit it was stealing, in a way, but everybody had been evacuated from Llanreath and I went round the backs of the houses, into the sheds. I picked up any pieces of material I could find and old screw-top bottles. I filled them with water and grabbed the apples and pears off the trees.

There was a pillowcase hanging on one of the lines and I took that, filled it up with all the fruit I could find and took it back to the tanks. And then I started distributing it to the men.

A huge plume of smoke hung over the town of Pembroke Dock.

JOHN WALSH

> It was hard work because the distance you had to run your hoses from the
> pumps was terrific. Sometimes I imagined all these tanks splitting and the oil
> running down onto Pembroke Dock and burning them all. We pumped up
> water from all the streams and brooks but mostly it came from the sea.

There was one frightening moment when the water supply ran dry – the tide had
gone out, leaving the pumps high and dry. It was not a mistake they made again.

Above all, though, it was the heat and burning oil continuously falling onto their
heads that the firemen remember. Most of them had nothing to wipe their faces
with, apart from the towels given out by the women of the town and by people like
Ted Owens.

TED OWENS

> I had bundles of rags for the boys to wipe their faces. But I kept some back for
> wiping the fruit I was giving out – it was all covered in oil and smut marks.

And it was not just the humans who suffered.

TED OWENS

> The local butcher had pigs in the next field down the road. And these pigs were
> screaming with fright. So they just opened the gates and away went the pigs,
> down Military Road, knocking everybody and anybody out of their way. I
> never saw a pig run as fast. They were black with all the smuts of oil falling.
> Because, oh, the flames were reaching right across the road, right into the
> fields on the other side.

HUBERT 'BUZZER' REYNOLDS

> One of the officers came up to me and said 'I understand, Reynolds, that you
> know a bit about pumps? Well, the pumps have stopped in the boat and we
> want you to go and have a look at them.' They were pumping water up from
> the Haven – four pumps sat in a boat out in the river, in Pennar Gut.
>
> Well, two or three blokes rowed me out to this boat where the pumps were.
> There was no water going through the hoses because these pumps had stopped.
> I was in the middle of putting petrol in, to get them going again, when Jerry
> dropped more bombs. It looked like a bunch of grapes coming down. The
> bombs landed right in the Gut. They didn't land on me, fortunately; they
> landed a couple of hundred yards away.
>
> I poured in the petrol to get the pumps working and then I got out of there.
> That was the end of the job as far as I was concerned: the water was back on,
> cooling the tanks.

The fire spread. Despite the efforts of the firemen, tank after tank erupted into a
mass of flames and smoke. Then, on 22nd August the fire claimed its first victims.
When the wall of one burning tank burst open it engulfed five Cardiff firemen –

Frederick George Davies, Clifford Miles, Ivor John Kilby, Trevor Charles Morgan and John Frederick Thomas.

Captain Tom Breakes had arrived from the Home Office only the day before, to take charge of the fire-fighting. He was called to give evidence at the Inquest and stated that 'there was a large burst of flame from the tank . . . . I saw no liquid, only a flame which seemed to engulf the men.'

JOHN WALSH

I was going off duty when the boys came to start work, five of them. I knew them all, they were from Cardiff. I said, 'Be careful, don't do anything daft,' because there were flames whipping around.

We went to bed that night and in the morning woke up to terrible news. 'We think there's been an accident,' one of the men said. 'Some of the boys have gone.' One of the tanks was burning, the oil was spurting out and I think what happened was that the tank cracked and the oil just poured out. It caught fire and they couldn't get away before the flames encircled them.

HUBERT 'BUZZER' REYNOLDS

Cliff and the other lads, they were such a team. They were wonderful, all of them the same ilk. It was a disaster, caused by some unknown means. Just – woof – imagine it, coming over the top like that. Our colleagues in 'the basement', in the bung as we called it, they couldn't get out.

JOHN WALSH

It's terrible to think that four of them had only just arrived at Pembroke Dock. I was shattered. I was sick. I was frightened. Every time I went back there I used to think, 'That could have been me. By the grace of God . . . That could have been me or Joe next door.'

One of them, Freddie Thomas, I worked with him when we were painters and decorators in Cardiff before we joined the fire service. And then all the rest, Cliffie Mills and the others, I knew them well from when they were training with the AFS. It was a personal loss. I remember thinking, 'What are their parents going to feel like?'

HUBERT 'BUZZER' REYNOLDS

Well, they say here today, gone tomorrow, but there's other ways of going. It was so sad, a real shocker.

After the tragedy we were sent home, some of us. But really you remained down there, thinking about it.

TED OWENS

I had the biggest row off my mother when I got home because when the Cardiff boys got burned somebody told her that I was one of the dead. I went berserk when I heard that. But she never told me who it was had said it. Never told me, kept it to herself.

WYNDHAM SCOURFIELD

I wasn't at the fire when the accident happened. I was off duty at the time. Of course the rumours started and, according to them, it was more than just the Cardiff boys. It shook us up, I can tell you.

JOHN WALSH

I cry sometimes when I think of it. When I go to a fire station today I think, 'Oh, look at the equipment you've got, compared to what we had.' Our engine that went to Pembroke Dock had an open body and you stood at the rail and rang the bell.

All I wore was what they called the fire tunic, just a tunic with two big red lapels. When you did your tunic up they were covered over but you opened them for ceremonies. We were dressed the same as policemen, no collars or ties. All we wore was the fire tunic and trousers with the red stripe down the side and leather boots. That's how I went to Pembroke Dock.

HUBERT 'BUZZER' REYNOLDS

There were hundreds of firemen there eventually. What else could they do but try to control it? The fire was just too big. There was another big oil-tank fire at Avonmouth later in the war. I was at that one, too, and we put it out. But don't forget, we'd advanced three or four years by then.

In the end, the fire at Pembroke Dock lasted for almost three weeks before the blaze suddenly went out. Eleven of the tanks had been lost, 38 million gallons of oil being burned or sucked up into the air and then deposited across the south Pembrokeshire landscape.

Pembroke Dock fire brigade, taken in 1947. Ted Owens is in the middle of the back row.

The Germans came back several times, using the smoke and flames to guide them to the target. Luckily their aim was poor. Yet the appearance of Dornier bombers and ME 109 fighters in the sky above Pembroke Dock invariably caused problems for the fire fighters.

TED OWENS

> I was issuing fruit to the boys and there was this officer, right outside the gate, standing on a fire engine. He had a big silver helmet on. I said, 'Excuse me, sir, that's a German plane over there, flying back and fore.' 'Do you think so, son?' he said. I said, 'Yes sir, that's a Dornier 117, nicknamed the Flying Pencil.' 'That's good enough for me, son,' he said and he rang the bell. Of course, all the rest heard it and they rang their bells too. And all the firemen came running out of the tank farm and into the field opposite.

Eventually, however, the fire was out. The firemen – and the people of Pembroke Dock – were able to breathe easily once more.

HUBERT 'BUZZER' REYNOLDS

> No-one had experienced anything like it before: balls of fire wrapped up in smoke, balls of smoke floating up into the sky. And the fall-out from the oil in the air was clinging to you all the time. The white chickens were black with oil. There was no difference, they were black like we were. We were covered in oil. It was just like rain coming down.

JOHN WALSH

> We woke up one morning and we couldn't believe our eyes. There was only a thin black pall of smoke. We couldn't believe it. The night crew came back and said, 'The flames have gone.' And that was it.

HUBERT 'BUZZER' REYNOLDS

> The people of Pembroke Dock, they really looked after us. They sacrificed their homes for us. I slept in St Patrick's Church Hall but some of the boys were taken into the houses. They laid on tea and coffee and food for us, all the time. The WRVS and the ladies of Pembroke Dock were marvellous.

WYNDHAM SCOURFIELD

> I didn't realize at first how inadequate our equipment was. It was just water, nothing else. Foam and all that stuff – well, we'd never even heard the names. That was brought down from Birmingham and places like that. To be honest, I think we were put in the background a bit when the bigger brigades arrived – all those boys in their kit and uniform. They looked like firemen – we looked like a bunch of amateurs. And to be honest, that's what we were. They were experienced men, no doubt about it. It wasn't a problem; we were very pleased. Without them I don't think we'd be here now.

JOHN WALSH

After the fire was out we still had to do our night shift. It was so eerie to think that we were walking through burned-out tanks. You just couldn't believe that a couple of days ago this was a huge bonfire.

When we were there, on the last night, there was another raid and we thought, 'Oh no, here we go again, they're going to bomb the rest of the tanks.' But they didn't.

In the aftermath of the fire there was considerable controversy. Why had such valuable oil tanks been left virtually undefended? What went wrong when the five Cardiff firemen died? And why was Pembroke Dock fire chief Arthur Morris – never a 'yes man' and always a fireman's fireman – overlooked in the awards that were liberally distributed in the aftermath of the disaster?

WYNDHAM SCOURFIELD

It was disgusting, absolutely disgusting. He was the man who carried the brunt of it all. Right from the beginning he knew what he was doing, what he was up against.

TED OWENS

Arthur Morris was a big man, a real old Pembrokeshire type. He plodded along, never raced – like the old saying goes, 'Always walk like a Dockyardie and you'll never go wrong.' But old 'Pop' Morris, he was a nice man, a very nice man.

He was there right from the start. I mean, it was him who realized how big the problem was and sent for the other brigades. But he never got a medal. The rest – from Milford, Swansea, Carmarthen, Llanelli – they all had medals. 'Pop' was the one who stayed there the longest and he got nothing. I could never understand that. Oh, we had all sorts of rows about that afterwards.

Arthur Morris (far right), Pembroke Dock's fire chief, in an off-duty moment.

For the Cardiff firemen it was a case of heading back home and getting on with the job.

JOHN WALSH

My mother had read about the fire but she never dreamed I was there. Not until I came home. Then the first thing she said to me was 'Where have you been? You haven't sent me a card!'

For the men of the Narberth brigade, the return home was not quite as triumphant as it should have been, however.

WYNDHAM SCOURFIELD

We were sent home on that final morning. The engine had been in use all the time and on the way back home it broke down in Templeton village. I'll never forget the Pembroke Dock fire – after the job was finished we had to walk the last two miles back into Narberth.

The last of the tanks – 11 of the 18 oil tanks were destroyed. South Pembs Golf Club now stands on the site.

Ted Owens became a full-time messenger for the Pembroke Dock fire brigade. It was a role he filled until, a few years later, he joined the Royal Marine Commandoes and fought with distinction in the final assault on Germany. His war, however, had almost come to an end some time before, during a heavy night raid on Pembroke Dock.

TED OWENS

I was standing in the doorway of the fire station. The engine was still inside. I said, 'Oh look, there's a parachute coming down.' I never thought it could be a land mine. The next thing it went off. The explosion blew me backwards, right to the back end of the fire engine. There were shelves there, all with tins of paint on. The whole lot came down on top of me – luckily none of them opened.

I was knocked out. They carried me in and put me onto one of the fold-up beds. The next thing I can remember is somebody washing my mouth with a sponge, trying to get rid of all the dust.

For the men who fought the Pembroke Dock blaze, the memory of those terrifying days will never leave them – nor will the memory of the men who made the ultimate sacrifice in the bid to save the tanks and people of Pembroke Dock.

### HUBERT 'BUZZER' REYNOLDS

I can still see it all, even now. I get a little bit emotional because it's often on my mind. Every year we have a Memorial Service down there and every time you meet old comrades there's another one less. It's sad, really.

### JOHN WALSH

In the whole of my fire service there was nothing to compare to the Pembroke Dock fire. Nothing.

Civic dignitaries, firemen and the four remaining fire fighters from 1940 at the 2003 Memorial Service to the Cardiff firemen who lost their lives.

'My sister Hilda ... was married while the great pall of black smoke reached across the Haven and into the far sky. In those days of coupons and clothes rationing, linen sheets and blankets were as precious as silver. My mother washed some of the blankets to remove their stiffness. She hung them on the clothesline ... It was a mistake that was marked on my sister's wedding present blankets for as long as they were in use. During the days that the fire burned, the sky rained minute droplets of oil and they rained on Hilda's wedding presents.'

Lord Parry of Neyland (quoted in *Inferno* by Vernon Scott)

# Chapter Five

# Fighting Back

There was scarcely a community in Wales that was not touched, in some way, by the war. Blackouts and ARP Wardens were soon commonplace, as was the sight of barrage balloons swinging like giant sausages in the air. Anti-aircraft guns and searchlights probing the night sky became a source of constant fascination for youngsters.

Yet, as the war progressed and as casualty lists began to grow, there came the gradual realization that, sometimes, people you knew and loved were never going to return from the conflict. MEIRIONA HUGHES remembers Brynrefail's first wartime casualty.

MEIRIONA HUGHES

I could see the telegraph boy, he came on his bicycle. He went up the street and turned left. He went to Mountain View and that was the house of Mrs Lewis – she'd lost her husband some years before. It was a telegram to say that her son who was in the Welsh Guards in France had been killed.

I remember when the telegraph boy came in afterwards and told us. It was terrible. We couldn't believe it. The first casualty. He was such a smart lad, all the girls used to – oh, Griff, he was very, very smart.

When the bad news was about a relative, it hit even harder. JOAN SMITH lived in the heart of dockland Cardiff.

JOAN SMITH

I remember one of my uncles, my Uncle Tiny, he came home from sea and came to our house to see my cousin. My cousin said, 'I'm just taking Tiny down to the Westgate Inn for a pint.' Then he walked him down to the dock gate to say goodbye.

That was the last time we ever saw Uncle Tiny because his ship sailed and three days later it arrived in Tilbury. They loaded up with ammunition and struck a mine just outside the harbour. That was it. He never came back.

The majority of our men were seamen and so many of them were killed. I don't think there was one street in the Bay where there weren't houses where seamen were killed.

At such times it was important to have the support of friends and relations. And although children like EDITH BODIN may not have always been able to understand why the war was raging they were certainly able to appreciate kindness when it was shown to them.

EDITH BODIN

> My Aunt Ada, she was a very tall Russian lady, very thin. And her husband, a big black feller, we called him Uncle Sam. They weren't relations really but we called everybody Uncle or Aunt.
>
> 'Get off to school!' Aunt Ada would say. 'Get up off that floor and get to school.' And we did, we took it and we went. We took it because she was looking out for us, looking after us. So we ran her messages and never stopped to think. We just went and got her papers or whatever she wanted. They were our neighbours.
>
> My father went to sea and brought things home. And it was all shared. People across the road, they went to sea and they shared everything too.

Sharing was important because rationing had been introduced relatively early in the war. Britain's farmers simply could not produce enough food for the whole country and so huge amounts had to be imported from the colonies and from America. The only way to bring in such vast amounts of food was by sea.

It was a perilous task. In the three months between March and May 1941, over 300 merchant ships were sunk by German submarines and by surface raiders like the *Scharnhorst* and *Gneisenau*. Over the next few months thousands of tons of allied shipping was sent to the bottom of the Atlantic as the U-boats tried to strangle Britain into submission.

Basic foodstuffs like flour, beef, grain and sugar quickly began to run short. The government response was rationing. As early as February 1940 all families had been expected to register with their local shops and soon even items like children's sweets were being restricted. Ration books were issued.

Butter, meat and fresh eggs were amongst the first items to be rationed. People were encouraged to use margarine and corned beef and even to cut back on the amount of food they ate. For people like ESTELLE CLARKE, who soon moved out into the country, there were benefits to living out of town.

ESTELLE CLARKE

> I think it was worse for people who were in the cities. Living in the country we were able to sneak the odd egg here and there. And of course we did grow all our own vegetables. We used to pick mushrooms in the fields and make a meal of them. It was all very, very dull, very restrictive, but it was something extra.

EDITH BODIN

> I can't remember actually seeing a ration book. I wasn't that involved, as a child. But definitely I can remember sharing. Perhaps it was a packet of tea. 'Oh, I've used up all my tea,' our neighbour would say. The answer was always 'Well, I can give you a spoonful.' I can clearly remember things like that.

ESTELLE CLARKE

We made do, really. We used to save sugar to make jam. Sugar in drinks and things like that, it was banned completely. Any little sugar you could save, that was it.

My mother was very fond of making wine and, inevitably, some of our sugar ration went into her wine. We hoarded little bits. We knew the people in the shop and occasionally they'd say, 'We've got some dried fruits coming in. Now I'm putting so much behind the counter for my friends but it will be shared out equally.' You'd get, perhaps, two ounces or maybe, if you were lucky, even four. And that would be it.

Variety of food was limited, too. Usually meals were about bulk, rather than exotic taste, SYLVIE BAILEY remembers.

"Ma says—May she borrow your cutest nightdress for twenty-eight days?"

Rationing was strict and when husbands came home on leave it could cause a few problems!

SYLVIE BAILEY

Food was very plain. You ate lots of vegetable stews, had dried eggs and bacon out of tins. Other than apples, pears and plums, fruit was very scarce. I was eight years old before I saw a banana.

We had cold cupboards in the garden or yards. I can still remember the smell of the milk in summer – it always seemed to be sour.

By the end of 1941, with the Battle of the Atlantic in full swing, rationing had become very stringent. By this time the weekly ration for one person consisted of 1 ounce of cheese, 4 ounces of butter, 2 ounces of tea, 12 ounces of sugar, 3 pints of milk, 1 packet of dried egg mix and one shilling's worth of meat (approximately worth £2.50 in modern currency). When Winston Churchill was shown the ration he commented that it seemed more than adequate to him. Unfortunately, Churchill thought it was the ration for one meal, not one week!

Fruit soon became a real luxury, as MARY ROSE remembers.

MARY ROSE

Oh, the shortage of food. What we missed most was bananas. We never had bananas all through the war. That's the thing that sticks in my mind. We never had bananas until after the war. It was a big thing then. These little things come to your mind, don't they?

ELUNED GILES from Caernarfon, BRYAN HOPE from Anglesey and DELYTH REES from Machynlleth also remember the privations only too well.

ELUNED GILES

In the beginning it wasn't so bad. There were still things floating about. But after a couple of years, how our parents managed to feed us I just don't know.

Some people couldn't get used to the rationing – like my grandmother. Every week she'd send us to the Co-op in Penygroes with a bit of paper – 'Tin of A1 salmon and a tin of peaches.' The shopkeeper, he'd say the same thing every week. 'Tell her she can get them at the end of the war.'

BRYAN HOPE

We used to bulk everything up with potatoes and carrots and turnips. Since sweets weren't available we used to spend practically all our money in the local chip shop. And in Amlwch they had this curious mix, known as a penny mix, where you had chips and mushy peas in a conical bag. All the juice and vinegar used to collect in the pointed end. I remember we used to suck these dry after we'd eaten the chips.

Food Flash

Rationing was a topic of daily discussion.

DELYTH REES

We were able to buy Ovaltine tablets, which were better than nothing. I can remember one occasion when we couldn't get any Ovaltine tablets, we had a penny to spend so we bought a penny Oxo cube and licked that.

BRYAN HOPE

One day a friend managed to pinch some potatoes off his mother. We borrowed a frying pan, took some bricks and built a fire. Then we started cooking chips. They were ghastly. They were greasy and quite raw, I suppose. But we ate them.

BOB EVANS, from Newport, remembers how, once the government began to ration sweets, it became almost a holy quest for children to find extra supplies of their favourite chocolate or sweet.

BOB EVANS

There's an area of Newport called the Handpost, just at the top of the Risca Road. We heard they were selling chocolate without coupons. So we piled in there and bought this stuff – with very dire results. It was laxative chocolate! Nobody knew; we were just small boys. We cleaned them out in about two hours – bicycles were coming from all over the place.

When he eventually discovered fruit, Bob Evans – like so many Welsh children – was amazed by what he saw.

BOB EVANS

I was given a banana. And I had no idea how to eat it. I thought, 'How do I attack this? You just pull the end off, don't you?'

It wasn't just food that was rationed. Petrol was soon in short supply and many cars found themselves abandoned and set up on blocks in dark garages for the duration of the war. And then, of course, there were shortages of things like cotton and linen. After 1st July, 1941, clothes rationing was introduced, people being given just 66 coupons to last them for twelve months.

SYLVIE BAILEY

Clothes were rationed like everything else. So casual clothes were unheard of. You were lucky, as a child, if you had one dress – and that would have been made by your mother. More than likely it would have come from an old dress of hers or your grandmother's. Swimming costumes were knitted up from old bits of wool. I can remember mine stretching down to my knees and nearly falling off when I went into the water.

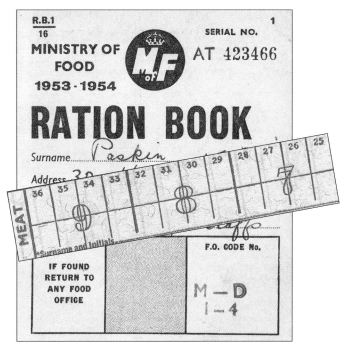

Men were forbidden to have turn-ups on their trousers and girls could not have pleats in their skirts. Old clothes were patched and darned over and over again – make do and mend, as it was called. One of the items not rationed was tobacco as it was felt that cigarettes were a morale booster. They were in short supply, however, as ELUNED GILES can testify.

ELUNED GILES

We thought this must be something special, if all these women were smoking. My mother had a sofa, an old-fashioned sofa with lumps in it. If you put your hand underneath you could pull out a lump of flock. We used to roll it up and make cigarettes with it. And it was vile, really vile. My sister lost all her hair because it just went up. But you know, most of us that were there smoking this stuff, we never smoked after!

With so many displaced people around – families who had been bombed out, wives following their husbands on a posting, soldiers who had been billeted in towns and villages – houses were often very crowded. Despite the problems of overcrowding, however, there were some compensations for young women like Estelle Clarke and Sylvie Bailey.

ESTELLE CLARKE

The house where I was staying in Swansea was full, every room. The family who owned it had a young child as well as two grown-up children in the forces. The sister-in-law had been bombed out so she and her husband were staying there. Then there were two 'fanny' drivers, ambulance drivers – one called Vivienne, the other from Canada – and then myself and a girl from London on the third floor.

So that was every room full – except the room where we ate and a small kitchen. When the boys came home, my husband and the husband of the girl from London, they used to sleep on the settee in the room where we ate because there was nowhere else for them. But we didn't care. We were just pleased to have them there.

SYLVIE BAILEY

Conditions were very primitive, I suppose. Toilets were out in the yard and you saved the newspaper, cut it into squares and hung it on the back of the door. You had a bath once a week. The radio was very popular and I can remember sitting in a big chair beside a blazing fire, in candlelight, listening to plays and music-hall programmes.

Enforcing laws about rationing was one of many tasks allocated to the police force during the war. Making sure that people kept their houses effectively blacked out at night and countering crime, wherever it might occur, were just two more of their many duties. And yet there were no more policemen on the beat. In fact, there were fewer than there had ever been, as HEDLEY ONIONS and JOHN GODFREY, both former police officers, remember only too well.

HEDLEY ONIONS

I would have gladly joined the services in any capacity but I had no option, the decision was taken away from me. It was compulsory for every serving police officer to register but as I was then classed as doing a job of national importance – supervising the Civil Defence organization of the area and training special constables and police auxiliaries – I was considered to be in a reserved occupation. So I just did the best job I could.

JOHN GODFREY

I was a cadet in Blaenavon police station during the war. There was a sergeant and three constables there. Every constable had to have a day off, and the sergeant too. So there were occasions during the week when I was the only person on duty. And I'd attend to everything that came in, over the telephone or people coming to the station. I was only sixteen. I'd wanted to become a policeman but I didn't want to wait until I was eighteen because, by that time, I'd have been called up into the army. So, as a way in, I became a police cadet.

HEDLEY ONIONS

I'd recently been promoted to sergeant at Neath. At the outbreak of war the police force was given the responsibility for training auxiliaries for civil defence. I was made Divisional Training Officer for all civil defence matters.

It meant training special constables, police war reservists – members of the public, similar to the Home Guard, who for various reasons, physical or otherwise, couldn't join the armed forces. So they joined the Civil Defence Service, as police reservists.

There were also some retired policemen, elderly men – the Dad's Army of the police force – who joined what was termed the First Police Reserve. They had a little background experience, obviously, although it had got a little rusty. But they were quite a help.

JOHN GODFREY

I didn't find there was much crime during the war. There were some thefts of coal from collieries and minor incidents like that but there was nothing too big. I like to think that perhaps all the people who used to be involved in that type of thing had been called up into the army.

Low crime rates or not, the war years were still a busy time for the police. There was so much to do – and much of it concerned tasks that, before 1939, had never entered anybody's head.

ELUNED GILES

There was a knock on the door one night and my mother went to open it. This policeman came straight past her, through the kitchen, mumbling something about a light. He went out into the back yard and fell flat on his back – he'd walked straight into the clothesline. Of course we thought it was great. He never knocked again.

JOHN GODFREY

As a cadet you worked in the police station, under the direction of the sergeant. You kept the books. I suppose you were actually the clerk of the station.

Any deaths in the armed forces and they'd send telegrams to the local police station first. They gave you 24-hours notice before the parents or families were informed. It was my job to deliver the telegrams when they came, to the people involved. I suppose I was fortunate in as much as I'd been brought up in Blaenavon and, fair to say, I probably knew everybody – or at least their families.

So, rather than go to the home to tell a wife that her husband had been killed, I'd go to a sister or a brother or someone like that. And I'd break the news to them. If there was nobody else I'd find a neighbour. I tried to do my best not to go alone but to be accompanied by somebody they knew when I broke the bad news.

Over 15,000 Welsh men and women were killed in the fighting during the Second World War and carrying such messages was a traumatic experience for a young sixteen-year-old in his first job.

JOHN GODFREY

For a young boy it was pretty horrible but, then, there was nobody else to do it. When you think about the number of people – soldiers, sailors, airmen – who were killed, perhaps once a week would be exaggerating, but certainly I'd have to go to people's houses three or four times a month to deliver bad news.

I didn't like doing it but it had to be done. It was something, that consideration, that was taught to me by other policemen. In those days policemen weren't allowed to live outside their area. So all of us lived in Blaenavon. We were part of the community.

HEDLEY ONIONS

Training the special constables was interesting. In the early stages they had no uniform. They did manage to find caps for them and armbands but that was all. As the war progressed they were gradually equipped with uniforms. To start with, we just had to give them basic training. It must have been hard for them.

They were a complete cross-section of the community. For example, I had a senior bank cashier seconded to me as an aide. I was really grateful for his ability in administration. Then I had miners, partly incapacitated, either by sight or some other problem, who weren't able to continue their normal work. In short, the specials were made up of young and old men who just didn't fulfil the requirements of the armed forces.

Sometimes the jobs that had to be done were specific and were directly related to the battles that were being fought in the skies above Wales. John Godfrey remembers one incident in particular that took place in May 1944.

JOHN GODFREY

I reported for duty at nine o'clock. We had a wonderful sergeant there then, Sergeant Haskell. I worked with him for three years and never once did he call me by my name. It was always 'Boy'.

Anyway, I went into the police station and he said, 'Don't take your cape off, boy. Come with me.' We got into his car and drove off towards Brynmawr. As we were approaching I could see smoke from what looked like a crashed aircraft. It seemed in quite good condition, I mean it hadn't broken up as such.

Now to get to the place we had to go to, Waunavon – it was the highest railway station in the country. We left the car there and walked along the railway track until we came to the place. It had crashed in a bog.

The aeroplane was a Halifax bomber, No. LK835, which had been involved in a routine cross-country flight when engine failure started a fire on board. The crew bailed out. In an article published in *The Police Pensioners Association Newsletter*, (September 2002) Ray Hapgood described the last few moments of the doomed bomber:-

Probing eyes in the valley towns of Blaina, Nantyglo and Brynmawr were drawn to a small patch of flickering light moving across the darkened sky. The Halifax was now only feet above the ground and narrowly missed the rooftops of a row of cottages near Milfraen Colliery.

Luck was with the inhabitants of the valley towns that night and, eventually, the plane crashed into a peat bog, close to the old Milfraen Colliery waste tip. All of the crew had managed to escape the stricken aircraft by parachute – landing in places like Abertillery and other valley communities. So when John Godfrey and his Sergeant arrived on the scene of the crash, their main task was damage limitation.

JOHN GODFREY

The Sergeant said, 'Boy, fill up the car boot with ammunition.' There were bandoliers of the stuff. So I filled up the boot – we had a real job to come out of the car park and get the car over the mountainside because it was so low down in the backside.

We got through to RAF St Athan and they sent a team up with a crane. But they weren't able to recover the plane because it was such boggy land. It was there, I suppose, for a year or something like that. Then, eventually, it disappeared into the bog. But for years afterwards, on very hot summer days, when the bog dried out, you could see the outline of the plane, there on the bog.

Mostly, however, the duties of a policeman at this time were more prosaic.

HEDLEY ONIONS

One of our special constables met one of his friends this particular evening and he was rather the worse for wear. The constable remonstrated with him, in a friendly manner, and of course the response of his friend was something like, 'Don't be so daft, Dai. Don't you remember? I'm your mate.'

So instead of locking him up for being drunk and disorderly the constable took him home – which is understandable, I suppose.

JOHN GODFREY

At the beginning of the war all the rifles and ammunition that people owned were confiscated. And they were brought to the police station. They were put in one of the cells. They were old muskets and flintlocks mainly – supposedly they were going to be returned after the war but I don't know what happened to them. In another part of the cells were two tea chests full of fireworks. They'd also been confiscated. You weren't allowed to have fireworks during the war.

HEDLEY ONIONS

Immediately the air-raid sirens sounded my duty, day or night, was to hurry to the Control Centre and liaise with the operational services – the fire service, ambulance, hospitals and so on.

Once, during the height of the bombing on Swansea, there was a series of what sounded like repetitive explosions – distant explosions. They were being recorded on the monitoring equipment. It turned out to be members of the Control Centre staff using the toilet.

Confusing flushing toilets with bombs may sound rather farcical but, in those far-off days of war, communication and technology were still in their infancy.

JOHN GODFREY

During those war years the police force had an understanding with the local bus services that they would carry letters for us. We would just give them to the driver. The bus company that ran between Pontypool, which was our headquarters, and Blaenavon was Ralphs Coaches from Brynmawr.

At eleven o'clock I had to go to the nearest bus station and the driver would give me my letters and I'd give him the ones for Pontypool. The last delivery would be four o'clock in the afternoon. I'd ring the cadet in Pontypool and say, 'Meet the half past four bus.' They saved us thousands of pounds doing that.

Preventing crime was still a major task for the police – or maybe not, as Hedley Onions remembers.

HEDLEY ONIONS

> On one occasion, in Neath, the house of a prominent man was broken into. The criminal searched in vain for money and left, largely empty-handed. Being a bit short of news the local newspaperman put a short column in the newspaper which said something like, 'Mr Blank's house at so-and-so address was broken into and the culprit left without stealing anything of importance. If he'd only looked in the teapot on the mantelpiece he would have been well rewarded.' The night the newspaper came out the criminal re-entered the house and stole the money. They never caught him.

JOHN GODFREY

> The ration books for the town of Blaenavon were kept in one of our cells. There was a ration office in the town, where you were given your new ration books, but they had no safe. So at five every night one of the male members of the office staff would come up with stacks of ration books and place them in the cell and lock them up. Nine o'clock next morning the same man would come back. We'd unlock the cell and he'd take them back to the office.

If all that sounds a bit like *Dad's Army* then it probably was. And yet the real *Dad's Army*, the Home Guard, was a very serious, if sometimes misunderstood, group of individuals who were to be the last bastion of defence should an invasion ever take place.

The Local Defence Volunteers were founded in May 1940, following the debacle at Dunkirk, when the call went out for recruits between the ages of 17 and 65 years to provide a volunteers army for home defence. Although the LDF soon changed its name to Home Guard, recruitment to the new force was fast and furious. In Llandudno two hundred people joined on the first day alone. By July 1940, over 1,500,000 volunteers had enlisted right across Great Britain. Nearly all of them had full-time jobs during the day, turning up to march and train at weekends or in the evenings.

In south Wales, in particular, the idea of joining the Home Guard had an immediate appeal. Many of the men in the valleys were employed in the mines, in reserved occupations,

**"COR! PARATROOPS!!"**

Fear of enemy paratroopers was one reason for the formation of the Home Guard in 1940.

and by joining the Home Guard they felt as if they were doing a little bit extra for the war effort. For people like HARRY RADCLIFFE and DANNY SEABOURNE, joining the Home Guard was something special.

HARRY RADCLIFFE

I was twenty when war broke out and I was called up. My mate, a month older than me, was called up in June. He went for his medical and was drafted straight away to India. I came up in the July batch, had my medical and got everything ready. My wife and I decided we'd get married in case anything happened to me. We got married in August 1940.

Then after France fell, they started sending all the miners back. If you were prepared to be an air gunner or flying, that was fine. But reserved occupations? It was back to the pits.

So I joined the Home Guard. I was out of one situation but I was also prepared to give myself to the defence of my country. An appeal went out for Local Defence Volunteers to go to the police station. We all went and I joined up there.

DANNY SEABOURNE

It came on the wireless that they wanted people to volunteer for the Home Guard. Well, I was about sixteen and working in the pit. All the youngsters joined the Home Guard because it was a little bit of fun, you know? Of course, in the valley there were plenty of volunteers because people hadn't been called up for the army. They were in a reserved occupation.

Part of the Nantymoel Home Guard – all of them, apart from the Sergeant on the right, were miners in Wyndham Colliery and Western Pit. Harry Radcliffe stands in the back row, second from the right.

HARRY RADCLIFFE

We were a rabble to start. My brother had a shotgun but the police confiscated that. We were drilling with sticks or broom handles or things like that, to get organised. As we became stronger, then we became more military-wise.

DANNY SEABOURNE

When we first joined the Home Guard we had broomsticks and you can imagine how they used to make fun of us. Then, later on, we had these cases of guns come in, and, of course, they were all covered in grease. We were all cleaning and boiling them out. The old fellas there, they were showing us how to do it like. We thought it was great. And then, when we had the bullets to go with the guns, that was marvellous.

An illustrated magazine features the Home Guard effort.

HARRY RADCLIFFE

We had our HQ in Commercial Street, Nantymoel, in an old house-cum-shop. Then our unit became too big so we were drafted down to the Church Hall in Pricetown. We were D Company and I was in Number 1 Squad, No. 1 Platoon. We were attached to the Welch Regiment.

You paraded, you saluted all the officers, proper regimental stuff. When we were issued with rifles, ammunition, bandoliers we went proper military style. No rabble. Everything was done as if you were in the regular army. It was no *Dad's Army*, it was proper regimental.

For the children of Wales, seeing the Home Guard on manoeuvres or exercises was great fun, as GAYNOR PUGH testifies.

GAYNOR PUGH

The Home Guard used to have exercises now and again, when perhaps Newtown would invade Aberdyfi. And then the scouts and the guides and the sea rangers would act as messengers on their bikes. They'd be hurtling back and forth between one group and another, a lovely excuse to go speeding on their bikes, I'm sure.

It was serious in as much as they were preparing for invasion. Yet it was fun too, and exciting. If the Home Guard decided to shoot at them, if they couldn't shout their identity number or the password that they had to use, they'd use a machine gun and shoot them. But the machine gun was a biscuit tin full of pebbles.

Biscuit tins full of pebbles couldn't hide the seriousness of the situation. After the summer of 1940, Britain stood alone against all-conquering Germany. An invasion was expected any day and people truly believed that the Home Guard might well make the difference between victory and defeat for this country.

HARRY RADCLIFFE

I'd be working afternoons in the colliery. On the Friday night I'd have to come home and if it was my guard night I'd go on duty. You weren't out every night but you had your nights of guard duty. We'd come up from the pit and we'd be on parade, say till eight or nine, drilling up on the mountains. We'd take a machine gun up with us and train on that. Or we'd go to Maesteg and practise throwing hand grenades.

After the bombing of Cardiff and Swansea, we had to be on top of the mountain by daybreak in case any parachutist dropped down. If Swansea or Cardiff or the Port Talbot steelworks were being bombed we'd get a message to patrol the top of the mountain. We'd have from the top of the Bwlch to Ogmore Vale. We covered both sides of the mountain, about ten of us, two threes and a four to cover that big area.

Sometimes, however, there were moments of humour to lighten the undoubted tension in the air.

DANNY SEABOURNE

There were some fellas a couple of miles away and all of a sudden we could see them running. We thought they were chasing a cow but they weren't. What it was, they'd shot the cow and they were following it down to the barn so they could tell the farmer what had happened.

HARRY RADCLIFFE

I was working afternoons but we had to go to HQ between eight and twelve, then go home and get ready for the afternoon shift.

This one morning the Company Sergeant Major told us, 'We've got a visitor coming over the Bwlch to inspect the units in south Wales.' He said, 'You've all had experience now in camouflage. I want you to go where you can see the road and get easy access to it for grenade-throwing or shooting.'

It must have been about eleven o'clock when this four-car convoy came over the Bwlch, down to what we called the Horseshoe Bend. From there we ambushed this general and he was so surprised that nobody had picked us up. He just didn't expect us to be there. It was great.

Our Sergeant Major called us all in and said, 'That was a really good achievement.' We would really have made a mess of that convoy if it had been for real. You could camouflage yourself in the mountains and nobody would see you.

The main job of the Home Guard was to defend the country against parachute assault, preventing airborne troops from gaining access to airfields, armament depots or dams and power stations. And whether the enemy came in ones, twos or a whole invasion force, the Home Guard was ready for them.

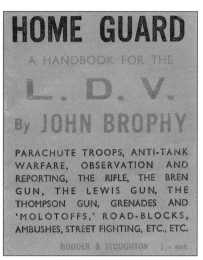

HARRY RADCLIFFE

> You were really proud to be seen carrying your rifle up the street, like any other soldier. My rifle was number 196; it was recorded against me and wouldn't ever go out of my hands. I wouldn't even hand it over to my officer. My rifle was kept behind the

The Home Guard Handbook.

> front door and my bandolier was hanging on a nail, ready by it. So as I was running out through the door I'd be picking up the rifle and bandolier and down the street I'd go.
>
> We were ready to give our lives. Whatever task they'd ask, you'd go one hundred percent towards achieving your goal. Whatever orders they'd give us, we'd go to the ultimate to try and complete the project.

Sometimes, however, good intentions were not enough. Sometimes accidents did happen.

DANNY SEABOURNE

> We were up the Pit Road by the reservoir. We were under cover, as part of a scheme, and we heard this rifle go off. Victor Moore, he was standing by me, well, lying by me, actually – 'Ooh I'm shot,' he said. And me and Noel Butler and a few others were laughing at him. But he had been shot, right through the calf of his leg.

As in almost everything else during the war years, it was the sense of comradeship that often kept people going.

HARRY RADCLIFFE

> Once we were dressed in uniform, as soldiers, and the Sergeants and the senior officers were explaining their positions to you, you started thinking, 'Well, we've got to get together and be a unit, not a rabble.' My squad, ten men, we all took it seriously. I was prepared to put my life on the line to defend my country.
>
> Wintertime, up on top of the mountain on patrol, it was really eerie. You'd hear the odd fox howling or something else dashing past. Other times it was a real treat to be up on top of the mountain at three or four in the morning.

Churchill reviewing Home Guard troops.

The Nantymoel units of the Home Guard came to be a highly efficient fighting force, armed with Vickers and Lewis machine guns, rifles and hand grenades. In the middle years of the war they were even equipped with anti-tank weapons.

Following the D-Day landings of June 1944, however, the threat of invasion evaporated and the order to 'Stand Down' the Home Guard was made on 3rd December, 1944. It came as a great surprise for many of the units, even though a hint had been given three months earlier when, on 6th September, the announcement had been made that there would be an end to all training for Home Guard Units.

The decision and order of Stand Down caused much resentment amongst the Home Guard who felt that they were being 'brushed away' now that they were no longer required.

HARRY RADCLIFFE

> We were called on parade and our captain, Captain Lloyd Jones, told us that we had ceased to function. We had to hand in our rifles, ammunition and everything else. We were just made redundant.

> The order had come in a tersely-worded signal – 'FALLOW GS and AA First November to be completed by 30th November.' Those eleven words just devastated four-and-a-half years of effort.

FALLOW was the code word chosen by the War Office to order Stand Down. GS stood for General Service (infantry) while AA meant Anti-Aircraft. It was over. Members of the Home Guard subsequently received the Defence Medal for their service on the Home Front during the war years but many felt that it was poor reward.

HARRY RADCLIFFE

It was an experience. All the Sergeants and corporals were ex-First World War men, all experienced soldiers. And to listen to some of them when we were on guard duty, well, it was a pleasure to listen to what they were saying.

We drilled with our rifles; boys who'd never handled a gun before had to be shown how to strip a gun and what else to do. It wasn't something you could do over-night. It took us months to perfect our actions.

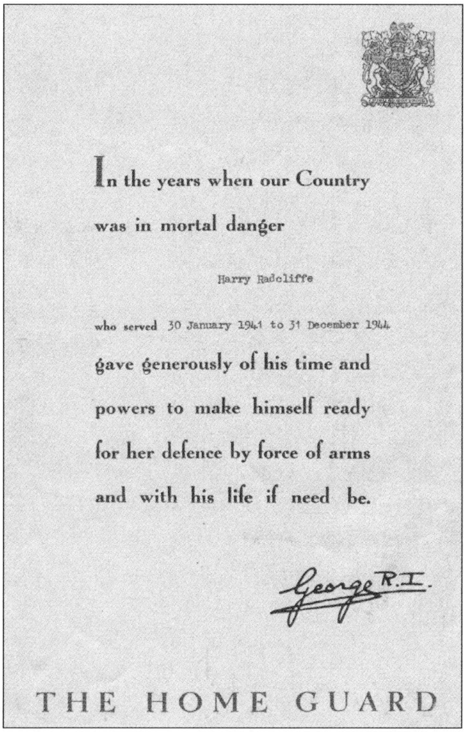

In the years when our Country was in mortal danger

Harry Radcliffe

who served 30 January 1941 to 31 December 1944 gave generously of his time and powers to make himself ready for her defence by force of arms and with his life if need be.

George R.I.

THE HOME GUARD

Harry Radcliffe's certificate from the King to mark his time in the Home Guard.

We just did our duty. We were prepared to do what we had to do if the occasion arose.

I missed it afterwards; going off and challenging other units on exercise. I missed all the adventure. It was an experience and at the end I missed it. I'd lost my butties.

'When we got to the Grammar School the war was still on and when we used to strip for PE, with only our shorts on … there was only one boy whose ribs weren't showing. The rest of us looked like Belsen. But we thought this was normal. We looked at him and thought he was the odd one out because you couldn't see his ribs.'

John Evans, Cwmparc

*Chapter Six*

# Women at War

The Second World War changed lives forever, not least the lives of women. In Britain at the start of the war only 39 women for every 100 men were engaged in regular employment. In the industrial belt of south Wales that ratio dropped as low as 16 to every 100. This was partly a cultural phenomenon but it was also a result of the Depression that had hit particularly hard in Wales. The Second World War brought important changes, however. During the next six years the number of the women employed in Wales more than doubled – slightly over 90,000 in 1939, well over 200,00 by 1945.

While some of these women served in the forces or the Land Army, the vast majority were engaged in war work at places like the Royal Ordnance Factories in Hirwaun, Bridgend and Glascoed. By 1942, these three ammunition factories had a combined workforce of over 60,000, the majority of the workers being women. And the ROF establishments were not alone. All over Wales, factories, privately owned or government run, were turning out ammunition, tanks or aeroplanes as fast as their production lines could operate.

HARRY HIGHMAN spent the second half of the war as an apprentice at the Royal Naval Propellant factory in Caerwent. He clearly remembers large numbers of women arriving at the factory each day, from places as far away as Monmouth, Brynmawr and Tredegar.

HARRY HIGHMAN

I think, during the war, there were something like six or seven thousand people working at Caerwent. We worked a three-shift system and thousands came in by bus every day. There was quite a fleet of buses, from vintage to 1937-38 variety. We even had some old London buses with the open staircase at the back. Everyone was engaged in the manufacture of cordite, propellant for naval guns.

There were a lot of women working there then, a lot of women. Before the war it was unusual for women to go out to work. But this factory was a godsend for them. A lot of them had husbands in the forces – so they were keen to see that what they made was good stuff.

Suddenly, it seemed, a whole new world had opened up for the women of Wales. It was not all plain sailing, however. MAISIE WILLIAMS was living in Pontypool at the time and, right from the start, she encountered a few problems about going out to work.

## MAISIE WILLIAMS

I'd put my name down to join the forces but my father was dead against it. He went down to the Labour Exchange and told them I wasn't to go. 'Don't worry,' they said, 'she's not of age yet.' When I reached the right age, they came up from the Labour Exchange to see if I could go. Dad said, 'No.' 'Well,' they said, 'if she doesn't go into the forces she's got to go into ammunition or the Land Army.' I went into ammunition.

Like Maisie Williams, ANNE HICKS and LINDA WESTERMAN were employed at ROF Glascoed, just outside Usk. For Linda, in particular, it was a significant change of direction.

OUT FOR VICTORY.

THE MUNITION GIRL.
"England expects every woman to do her duty."

The Munition Girl.

## LINDA WESTERMAN

I was working in a hotel in Bournemouth when war broke out. I was a waitress there. One day the boss came and said, 'You girls have got to finish.' We looked at him. 'This isn't work of national importance,' he said. So we came home and had to register for this work of national importance. They sent me out to the Dump at Glascoed.

## ANNE HICKS

I went there after I had my baby. My husband went into the forces and I went there when my boy was two years old. Because the army pay was nothing. I went into the factory, working on the bombs – two-pounders, RDX and all that.

RDX was a component used in bomb manufacture, known to cause damage to the nervous system, albeit only at high concentrations. However, even lower concentrations could sometimes cause a carcinogen. But RDX wasn't the only potential problem at Glascoed.

## MAISIE WILLIAMS

There were some very nasty accidents. We were there one morning and there was a terrific explosion. When you gauge a shell you knock it with a rubber hammer but some people just knocked it with another shell. This day it caused an explosion. Oh, there were a few people killed down there. It was quite dangerous.

LINDA WESTERMAN

You had to be very careful with TNT – liquid TNT. It was terrible. I had a dose of TNT poisoning and it was really bad. They took me off the TNT, for months, until I got it out of my system. And when I got back they said, 'You can go down to cordite.' Well, that was even worse – it used to give you a terrible headache.

ANNE HICKS

Your hair used to go yellow – all different colours, really – when you were working with TNT. When I was in RDX, it had to be heated in a big pan, like dough. I was in the shop one night and a shell went off. It just opened up like a tulip, bent all the steel that was inside. And that was only a two-pounder.

LINDA WESTERMAN

One day we had an explosion on Section One. That was terrible. I knew the two men; they only went from one shop to another to get something. One man hit the bottom of the shell – he'd been warned against it. But he hit it anyway and up it went. They were blown to smithereens.

Conditions in the factory were never easy – quite apart from the danger. And security was always high.

ANNE HICKS

We used to open the doors at night. Of course, you couldn't have lights on. We used to sit on the floor, open the doors so there was some air coming through and pull the blind down. Otherwise you'd never stick the heat or the smell.

LINDA WESTERMAN

They'd search you when you went in. Then into the danger area and you'd be searched again. You'd go into the boot house and leave your cigarettes and lighters and all that. You'd collect them on the way out. They'd search your hair for clips. Your wedding ring had to be covered or taken off and you couldn't take in sweets or chewing gum. When you went into TNT or shellac you had to put make-up on. It was the best Max Factor liquid to protect your skin.

The compensation, of course, came in the money that was earned. Many miners resented the wages that the women workers were now bringing home, even though it was still considerably less than male factory workers. The weekly wage of an unskilled female munitions worker was around £4, equivalent to a skilled surface worker in the mining industry and higher than most underground workers.

MAISIE WILLIAMS

Our lives changed. We had a different outlook on things. Whereas before, regarding clothes, you had a best thing and you didn't put that on during the

week, now all that changed. You lived for the day because you didn't know
what was going to happen. We'd never seen such money. I can remember my
father working all week for £2.10, to keep a family. After a while they
transferred me to Coventry – I can't remember why. But I got paid with my
first £5 note. The big white ones. You had to write your name and address on
them before you could spend them.

By 1942, over half the war workers in Wales were women and there were urgent
calls to give priority to unemployed men when it came to filling vacancies in the
ROF factories. It made little difference, causing one ex-miner to tell *The Western
Mail*, in March 1943, that: 'I'm one of the unemployables . . . since my old woman's
been working my life has been just hell.'
     VERA SMITH worked in a factory at Treforest, producing long belts of machine-
gun bullets. When she reached a production target of 8000 a day her pay increased.

VERA SMITH
     I would come home, very proud of how much money I was earning. I
     happened to mention it to my father and he didn't like it at all. Because, of
     course, he wasn't earning anything like that. And, I mean, my job was easy
     compared to what he was doing because he was working underground. He was
     quite angry about it.

Some people regarded women who worked in the factories as having low moral
standards and the factories themselves as places where all manner of debauchery
went on. It is a point of view that is strenuously denied by the women themselves
and debases the work that the women did in the factories. Many of them had
husbands in the forces. For the single women, while the work was undoubtedly
hard, it was important that, when off duty, there were opportunities to let their hair
down.

MAISIE WILLIAMS
     During the evenings there was plenty of dancing – places like the Palais de
     Dance in Pontypool. When we were on afternoon shifts, we'd often get a lift
     home in one of the vans, get into Pontypool and have the last three dances.
     Then get someone to take us home. But that was it. I used to be nervous, shy.
     Working like that, it broadened me out, I think.

LINDA WESTERMAN
     One night, my friend and I were going past one of the air-raid shelters and we
     heard this moaning and groaning. And there was this woman having a baby.
     'You go for the nurse,' I said to my friend. It was a regular occurrence down
     there – some would always leave it to the last minute. There were a lot of
     babies born to women working till the last minute.

Sometimes danger came from outside the factories. HARRY HIGHMAN worked at Caerwent during the war, only moving to Glascoed after hostilities ended. Nevertheless, he still remembers one aerial attack on the Usk factory.

HARRY HIGHMAN

I think it was November 1940 or 1941. A German plane came across country, looking for Filton near Bristol, where they made aero engines. He came in low on a very misty day, at about 200 feet. He came over Usk and followed the railway line. Then he saw all the buildings, people walking on the clearways and waving to him – 'It's one of ours up there.'

LINDA WESTERMAN

Everyone was going to their break. We all wore white overalls, white turbans or hats. This German came down and we were all waving. Until he opened fire. I went sprawling. Somebody chucked me over onto the grass. And I said, 'I'm in a hell of a mess here.' And the bloke said, 'Aye, and you'd have been in a worse bloody mess if I hadn't chucked you over there.'

ANNE HICKS

That's when it hit you, what was going on. All the guns around the Dump, when they realised what was happening, they opened fire. But they never troubled him. One of our women workers caught a piece of shrapnel in her breast but there were no deaths. One man was building the toilets and he was buried up to his neck in earth.

HARRY HIGMAN

He dropped, I think, about twelve bombs and machine-gunned the area. He destroyed one or two buildings, then off he flew.

Such incidents were rare. Mostly people just got on with the job and enjoyed what they were doing. They were being well paid and knew that they were also helping their country in a time of crisis. There was still the opportunity for a little fun, however – there needed to be, because the war and its consequences were ever present.

MAISIE WILLIAMS

What we used to do was we'd write our names and addresses on slips of paper and drop them in the ammunition boxes. The men at the front, they'd open the boxes and the papers would be stuck down between the bombs. We had quite a lot of replies. We kept contact with a few but, as the years went on, it stopped. A lot of their letters were censored anyway and I expect ours were as well.

LINDA WESTERMAN

I lost my two brothers and my husband, all within eleven months of each other. My husband was called up from the Dump and I had to stay there working. He was killed six months before my daughter was born.

It made you grow up, quick. We were only young girls but you had to grow up quick then.

Work in the Royal Ordnance Factories was not the only employment available to women at this time. CHRISTINE JONES became a telephone engineer in the Abergavenny area shortly after war broke out.

CHRISTINE JONES

I'd been working in Bristol, as a nurse. But then the housekeeper died at home and I came back. I went down to the Labour Exchange and the man there said, 'Would you like to go round putting in telephones?'

Christine was unsure at first – it all seemed so complicated. The man at the Labour Exchange promised her a van and sent her off to see the inspector. She was given the job.

CHRISTINE JONES

The first thing I did was to go to Abergavenny Castle. They showed me the switchboard and the wires. I thought, 'Oh dear.' Mr Gage was the engineer and he trained me.

When I was training I went to work one morning and Mr Gage said, 'I was called out in the night but I didn't bother calling you.' That was fine but then he said, 'Do you know who was at Aber last night? Churchill. I went to the Great Western station and he was there on the train. I put a phone in for him.'

Christine Jones may have missed the Prime Minister but she did get the chance to see several other famous faces during her time as a telephone engineer.

CHRISTINE JONES

I went to Gilwern Hospital one day and was on this ladder against a pole. I was putting in the wire and Jimmy Cagney walked by. James Cagney. I lodged in Abergavenny at the time and the children where I was staying said, 'Why didn't you get his autograph?' He hadn't seen me, just walked by with two American soldiers each side. I never thought of it until I got home and the children asked.

Sometimes the people that she met were a lot less appealing than American film stars.

CHRISTINE JONES

Once I saw Hess. Really. We were up at this big house and there was a soldier with a gun. I was walking down and Mr Gage was getting his equipment ready to put the phones in. This soldier went to catch hold of me, he lifted me up in the air to a window. 'What do you think you're doing?' said Mr Gage. 'Cut it out.' The soldier said, 'I'll tell you what I'm doing. I'm trying to show her Hess.' It was Rudolph Hess, there in the room. We put a phone in for him.

Large numbers of American soldiers were billeted in the Abergavenny area, prior to the D-Day landings. Christine Jones remembers the time very well, in particular the build-up to the Normandy landings.

CHRISTINE JONES

Abergavenny was full of Yanks then. Every night. They all wanted to know where the dances were. We used to have concerts every Sunday night in the Town Hall and there were dances every Saturday. In the Angel they had a place called a Doughnut Dugout. Abergavenny was marvellous then, they'd never seen anything like it.

But I remember the day before D-Day. I was doing the wiring and the Yanks were on the phones. They were on about ships and I could hear them saying things like, 'This'll be it, then,' or 'Zero Hour'. I thought there's something going on. I'm sure it was a Monday and then, on the Tuesday: D-Day. Abergavenny was suddenly like a ghost town. Nobody there at all.

The Women's Land Army was originally set up to help food production in 1917 but after the armistice of 1918 was allowed to disband. By 1938, however, British agriculture was in a parlous state with nearly 70% of the country's food having to be imported – in direct contrast with Nazi Germany where nearly all its food requirements were produced at home.

The idea of using women to work on the land, in an effort to increase production, was discussed at high levels as early as April 1938. Yet it was only after considerable pressure from Lady Denman, who had assisted Dame Meriel Talbot in setting up the original Land Army during the First World War, that plans and discussions were finally transferred into action.

Recruiting poster for the Women's Land Army.          *(Robert Opie collection)*

Administered by the War Agricultural Committee (quickly shortened to WARAG), the Women's Land Army was re-formed on 1st June, 1939, before war had begun, and by the end of the year, four-and-a-half thousand young women had been placed on farms throughout Britain. By the end of May 1940 that figure had risen to 6000 and, before the Land Army was finally disbanded in November 1950, the organisation would come to number some 80,000 women and girls.

The aim of the Land Army was admirably summed up in July 1941 when a further two million women were called upon by the government to register for national service – to stop the practice of men filling jobs that could ostensibly be carried out by women.

Within the Land Army there were a number of specialist fields. Women could opt for farming, fruit growing, market gardening, forestry, timber measures (sawmills etc.) or greenhouse work. Within these specialities they did things like driving tractors, running milk rounds, tending to sheep or cattle and looking after poultry.

The Land Army organisation published its own magazine, *The Land Girl*, and issued a Handbook to all new entrants. The Handbook offered all sorts of advice to newcomers, some practical, some not:-

> Town girls on the whole use more make-up than country girls. The Women's Land Army volunteer should therefore be prepared to 'tone down' her lips, complexion and nails.
>
> To make gum boots slip on and off easily, sprinkle French chalk inside the gum boots from time to time.

The Land Army even had its own song, although quite how many women knew or sang the words is questionable.

> We're girls, girls of the land are we.
> When we're working we're happy and free,
> We work for its pleasure,
> We've no time for leisure,
> So join in the Land Army.

JOAN MACDONALD and DORIS CURTIS were two young women who enlisted in the Land Army quite early on.

JOAN MACDONALD

> I went to the school of commerce at Pontypridd and did shorthand and typing. We had an aunt living in Gloucester and as there was lots of work there I went up to Gloucester for a few years. My friend Florence, from Tenby, came up and joined me.
>
> Because she was four years older than me she had to do work in the evenings, for the war effort. She either had to join the fire service for evening work or the ambulance service. She said she wouldn't like to do that. So we decided to join the Land Army.

DORIS CURTIS

> There was a point in the war when you were called up and had to go where they sent you. My friend and I didn't want to go into the army or the RAF or anything like that so we settled on the Land Army.
>
> We got our uniforms in Chester and we came down – well, they said Carmarthen; I thought it was Caernarfon. I mean, my father was from Bangor and I'd spent so much of my youth there, just up the road from Caernarfon. I thought well, that's great. And then we ended up at Carmarthen.

JOAN MACDONALD

For our first farm they sent us to Cowbridge. Florence wasn't very experienced
but me, being a farmer's daughter, I'd been on the farm. I could milk and do
most things. For the first six weeks the government paid the farmer to train
you and Florence was supposed to be trained. It was terribly hard, you know,
trying to pitch up hay and things like that. She didn't have a clue.

The farmer wanted to keep me but not Florence. Anyway, we gave in our
notice, which we shouldn't have done really. Then we were both sent to
Pentrebane Farm at St Fagans and we were there for the next four years. It was
a lovely farm. Five hundred acres, nine Land Army Girls plus the men. I think
there were 21 of us working on the farm. We were very happy there.

DORIS CURTIS

When we got to Carmarthen station there was a lorry waiting for us. We all
piled in and they took us to the hostel. There were about eight cubicles with
four beds in each cubicle. I think there were 28 of us there eventually but we
were the first ones there, you see.

JOAN MACDONALD

There were only lanterns in the sheds and many times, when passing through
the barn from one cowshed to another, the young boys would jump out of the
shadows and scare us. One morning I thought I'd have a joke on them. I waited

The Countess of Plymouth presents Good Service Badges and Proficiency Certificates to Glamorgan
volunteers – Joan MacDonald is seen receiving her award.

until I heard someone approach and sprang out, shouting 'Boo!' It was the Boss. He spilled some of the milk from his bucket and I had to go to the house after breakfast for a reprimand.

Land Army girls like Joan Macdonald were lucky if they lived on the farms. Many of the volunteers had to stay in specially created hostels, as BETTY DAVIES remembers.

BETTY DAVIES
The food in the hostels was terrible. I don't say they were all the same but the one we were in was terrible. We didn't have enough to eat – all we had was turnips and potatoes. We never saw a piece of bacon or meat. It was hard work, back-breaking. Cold sheets and oil lamps. And our water was pumped from the brook.

Prunes for breakfast, turnips and tatties for dinner. Bread and jam? I've never seen bread curl like ours did. Bread and jam to go out in the field to work. We used to light a big bonfire in the middle of the field. We'd have a twig, put our jam sandwiches on the end of it and toast them over the fire.

DORIS CURTIS
We had a warden in charge of our hostel. She was very strict. You had to be in by ten, no messing. If you weren't there the doors were locked. Of course, there were always ways around it and the warden knew what was going on. But that was the rule – ten o'clock, door locked.

We only had three bathrooms in the hostel so, after a day out on the farms, you had to get back quickly. The first crowd back got all the hot water. But it was fun. Let's face it, twenty odd girls together? We had a laugh. We all got on well together.

The jobs in the fields and on the farms were new and often very different from anything any of them had ever done before.

DORIS CURTIS
The first job we had to do was clear land at Llanddowror, clearing gorse bushes and trees, then burning them. I was driving the tractor. I'd never driven anything before but I had to drive that tractor with great thick chains wrapped around this tree trunk. You had to jerk the trunk out but the chain snapped and went straight into my back. It was just one of those things. You didn't complain, you just got on with the job.

I learned to drive in the Land Army. One man, an oldish chap working for the WARAG, he said 'Right Doris, get in the van and drive to Llandeilo.' I mean, that was it. Now I'd driven the tractors but I didn't know the first thing about driving cars or vans. But I drove on the old road to Llandeilo and never thought much about it. That was my introduction to driving.

A group of Land Army girls in Carmarthenshire. Doris Curtis is second from the left, front row.

JOAN MACDONALD

Les, the young boy who was with us, he didn't have a watch. We were miles away but we could see each other. The way I used to call him in for dinner or for milking was, on the old Fordson tractor, if you pulled the choke right out for a few minutes, it gave off rings of smoke. I'd send up signals to tell him to come in for his dinner.

BETTY DAVIES

It was a different life altogether. Most of the Land Girls used to come with painted nails when they first joined up – and nylons. But they soon had to get rid of all that once they were out in the muck, on the land.

You'd be out in all weathers and winds, on the tractor. And there were no cabs on them in those days to keep you dry. I'd never go back, ever, to those days again. They were happy days but, looking back now, I'd never go back.

There was no doubt that the life was much harder than anyone had ever imagined. If a girl was on her own on a farm, rather than in a hostel or billeted with other Land Girls, it could be too much to bear. Joan MacDonald's sister, GWYNETH JENKINS, remembers the awful loneliness of it all.

GWYNETH JENKINS

I was by myself on a farm at Llantwit Major. The farmer was a bachelor and there weren't any other girls around. It was my first time away from home and I wasn't really happy on the farm. I felt so lonely.

One night I went to the pictures in Bridgend and missed the last train. Eventually I got back to the farm and tried the door but it was locked. So I hid in the barn for a while. The farmer came out to look for me, to be fair, but I didn't show. He lit a torch and looked around but he didn't find me. Then I took my bike and I went home. In the morning I got in touch with the Land Army and told them I wasn't going back.

Some of the Land Army girls were sent to serve in the Timber Corps – the Lumber Jills, as they soon became known. For some of them, like ANN HUGHES, it wasn't a matter of choice. They simply went where they were sent.

ANN HUGHES

I didn't know I was going to work in the forestry. I just joined the Land Army and then I was sent to Tre'r-ddôl, between Machynlleth and Aberystwyth. We were there chopping down trees. It was as simple as that.

We had several men who were lumberjacks, local men. We went up into the woods and they showed us how to make a 'cheese' in the tree – chop a piece out of one side, then go to the other side and chop until the tree falls down. But you had to shout 'Timber!'

Others, like LYN WHITTOW, made a deliberate choice about their speciality

LYN WHITTOW

My mother not wanting me to leave home, I went to work in a factory near Merthyr. I worked there for six months but after the bombing in Cardiff and working in a noisy factory it upset me so much that I pleaded with my mother to let me join the Land Army.

When I went to the recruiting office there was a girl dressed in the Land Army uniform but with a green beret. I was curious and enquired about the reason. She must have been a very good sales woman because I ended up joining the Women's Timber Corps, not really knowing what it was all about.

ANN HUGHES

Really, all the men were very helpful. But one day I had a terrible fright when we were walking up a steep hill. We had horses to drag the trees and one of the men said, 'Do you want a ride?' I said, 'Oh, yes.' I jumped on – no saddle or anything – got hold of the horse's mane and they slapped its backside. Off I went, down the hill. How I stayed on I'll never know. But I do know I was crying when I got to the bottom.

LYN WHITTOW

It was a man's job, really, too hard for girls. But it was our job. We were sent there, we had to do it – and we did. It was so different. We had never picked up anything heavier than a hairbrush and now there we were, swinging a long seven-pound axe or a fourteen-pound sledge-hammer all day.

We even had to sharpen our own axes. There was an old grindstone, hand-driven. One girl would turn the handle and we'd sharpen and hone our axes and saws. When we finished work for the day, we'd push them under a hedge and next morning we'd trim them up before we started work again. It wasn't too bad in the spring and summer but in the winter there was ice and frost. Then it wasn't quite so easy.

ANN HUGHES

I had a wonderful experience. I'd only been there a few weeks when one of the farm workers – he was just a boy then – asked me if I'd like to see a foal born. And that, to a girl from the city, well it was exhilarating.

New experiences were all part of the life of a Land Army girl. Simply walking in the countryside was something that many of the volunteers had never done before.

ANN HUGHES

There was no transport at all. The little bungalow I lived in was seven miles away from work. I walked it in the morning and back home again at night, in rain or hail or snow. I loved walking. I'd always been a great walker but I'm sure that many of those girls hadn't walked very far at all. It was a great change for them.

JOAN MACDONALD

Les, the young boy on our farm, he was always joking. We'd go out to plough and, of course, the furrows would be absolutely straight. But he would say, 'Oh, I picked up some rabbits this morning in that furrow you ploughed.' 'How did you do that, Les?' we'd say. 'Well, they'd knocked their brains out because it was so crooked, running up the furrow.' Or he'd tell the girls that the way to catch a rabbit was to go out to the arable land where there was a big stone. 'Put pepper on it,' he'd say, 'and the rabbits will sneeze and knock their brains out.'

WOMEN'S LAND ARMY PROFICIENCY CERTIFICATE.

THIS IS TO CERTIFY THAT

Miss J. C. Jenkins.          W.L.A. No. 100672.

HAS BEEN AWARDED A PROFICIENCY BADGE

IN Milking and Dairy Work.

AND HAS GAINED DISTINCTION.

Date February 1944          Signed C. Denman.

on behalf of the Women's Land Army.

A Proficiency certificate in Milking and Dairy Work, presented to Joan MacDonald (Joan Jenkins as she then was) in January 1944.

### GWYNETH JENKINS

After I ran away from the farm at Llantwit Major they said I had to go back to work out my notice. And the farmer, he wasn't nasty, he just said, 'Get yourself up here and get on with the job.'

I worked my week, then I went to another farm. As soon as I went through the door, well, it was lovely. It was a young family, they had two little children, a boy and a girl. I was there for two years and was extremely happy there.

### DORIS CURTIS

One of the girls, she was a cheeky sort. She wouldn't do anything, you know. She'd try to get out of everything. Well, this day, our forewoman, Edith Lewis, just turned her upside down and slapped her backside. We all had a laugh at that, treated it as a bit of a joke.

### LYN WHITTOW

At lunchtimes we'd sit with the sandwiches that our landladies had given us. Every day I had cheese and I got so tired of it. Except, one day, I was surprised to find meat in there. I swapped one of mine with a girl called Brenda. I was about to take a bite out of another of my sandwiches when I wondered what type of meat it was. So I opened it up and saw what I thought was a lump of fat – until it moved. It was a massive half-inch long maggot, squirming around. Brenda just ran around screaming, 'I've eaten a maggot!'

Although estimates taken in 1940 stated that there was a shortfall of approximately 50,000 agricultural workers, the Women's Land Army soon began to make great inroads into the deficit. By the spring of that year, over two million new acres were under the plough and Land Army girls were happily filling jobs of men who had gone into the armed forces, either through conscription or by volunteering for service.

On occasions, the work of the Land Girls was more than a little dangerous.

### LYN WHITTOW

There was a girl I hadn't worked with before but we were paired together for some reason. I always kept my axe beautifully honed, you know, like a razor's edge. We were taking it in turns to cut this tree. Some of the trees had a lot of sap inside them and it made everything a bit slippery.

This other girl, she asked me if she could borrow my axe because hers wasn't very good. She took the down stroke, the axe turned in her hand because of the sap and came down on her right eyebrow. Blood squirted everywhere. She was taken off to hospital.

Some time later we were working together again. We were always warned never to stand astride a log and come down with an axe. She got hold of the axe and it went through her foot. Hospital again.

### JOAN MACDONALD

One of the girls there with us on the farm, she had an accident in the threshing drum. She had her leg off. Lots of girls had nasty accidents in those drums.

In general, however, the experience of working as a Land Army volunteer was something that the women will never forget. It was, quite simply, a marvellous memory.

DORIS CURTIS

Oh, I wouldn't have missed it. It taught me a lot in so many ways. You learned to live with other people and, let's be honest, some of those farmers weren't very nice. Some of them were downright nasty. You learned to stick up for yourself. Normally, back at home, I wasn't like that but you just had to do it.

JOAN MACDONALD

All in all, we had a pretty good time. The food left a lot to be desired but, then, they were cooking for twenty people at a time. We slept on camp beds in the cottage behind the farm and we were quite happy. You met all these lovely girls, you worked hard. It was a happy time although it was sad, too, because of the war. Sad but happy days as well.

Land Army girls pose with their farmer.

A little residue of bitterness remains, however, not about the Land Army or the experience but about how the volunteers were treated, both during and after the war.

ANN HUGHES

I felt that nobody had looked after us much during the war. I don't ever remember anybody coming to say, 'Are you happy in your digs? Do you get enough to eat?' In one place I had a herring and bread-and-butter pudding every night for six months! They sent me to Builth Wells, into a very funny hostel. I used to go to church, for six weeks I went, in my uniform, and not a soul spoke to me.

Now, at last, the Bevin Boys are invited to march on Remembrance Sunday but there isn't a mention of the Land Army. I always feel that's rather bad.

DORIS CURTIS

We weren't treated like the ATS or anyone. We never had travel warrants or anything. The first six months they wouldn't even let us go home. I think they were afraid we wouldn't come back. No, we weren't treated like the ATS. We weren't a service like them. That was the only thing we didn't agree with, you know. I watch them march now on Remembrance Sunday, on the television. There are no Land Army girls and I don't know why.

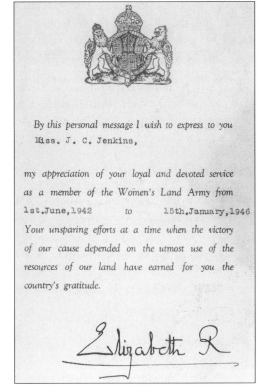

By this personal message I wish to express to you Miss. J. C. Jenkins,

my appreciation of your loyal and devoted service as a member of the Women's Land Army from 1st.June,1942    to    15th.January,1946 Your unsparing efforts at a time when the victory of our cause depended on the utmost use of the resources of our land have earned for you the country's gratitude.

*Elizabeth R*

Certificate from the Queen, commemorating service in the Land Army.

In addition to factory work and the Land Army a great number of Welsh women were conscripted into or volunteered for service in the ATS, the WAAF or the WRNS. Many of these newly-enlisted service women actually served in Wales. BARBARA JONES, after an initial period of training in London, found herself at Pwllheli in north Wales.

BARBARA JONES

I joined the WRNS because you could go and be interviewed when you were seventeen and a quarter. With the ATS and the WAAF you had to be seventeen and a half before they'd look at you. I know it's awful but I didn't want the war to end until I was old enough to join up. I just wanted to do something. You had propaganda posters everywhere. You all had to do your bit.

After training, my first job was serving and waiting in the Ward Room, a huge place at HMS *Glendower*, which was the Butlins Holiday Camp in north Wales.

For MARY PHILLIPS it was the WAAF, the Women's Auxiliary Air Force, that had an immediate appeal. And she, too, found herself serving close to home in Wales.

MARY PHILLIPS

I suppose I was happy to join the WAAF because of the glamour of the RAF. It wasn't all that long after the Battle of Britain and all those flyers, well, they were like heroes to us then. I trained at Morecambe and eventually they sent me to Talbenny, an aerodrome in Pembrokeshire. That was good because it was only a short distance from my home in Pembroke Dock. It meant I could cycle home at weekends or whenever I could get a pass.

BARBARA JONES

I can't remember being homesick. Everything was so different and you were with lots of different people. You were helping to win the war. 'Free a man for the fleet' was the slogan, because the WRNS weren't sea-going then.

Soldiers had to learn to make room for women in the forces.

MARY PHILLIPS

I was serving and waiting in the office's mess. They were lovely blokes, all really nice and friendly. No snobbishness or anything like that. Well, I suppose being a snob was the last thing on their minds, what with the war and all.

For DENISE LLEWELLYN, the Women's Royal Naval Service was attractive because of their smart uniform. When she joined up, however, she realized to her horror that she might have got herself deeper into trouble than she had ever imagined.

DENISE LLEWELLYN

On my Welsh Certificate of Education they noticed that I'd got a credit in Science and Maths. But that was only because I'd swotted it up. I really didn't know anything about them. Anyway, I was called to see if I was suitable to be a radio mechanic. There was a Bunsen burner and a soldering iron and a block of wood with a little bulb fixed into it. And a couple of broken electrical wires.

I looked at these with horror – well, I had no idea what I had to do with them. The WRNS officer explained. She wanted us to solder the wires together and do whatever you had to do to make the bulb come on. And in no time at all bulbs were lighting up all over the laboratory. I was still sitting and looking at mine. I had not the faintest idea. I felt so depressed and thought, 'Oh, they'll just send me back.'

Next day the officer sent for me and said, 'I notice you've got extremely neat, clear writing.' She handed me a poem and I wrote it out in front of her. She said, 'This is just what we're looking for. We need people who can write in small writing but it must be very clear because you'll have to write between the lines.'

I thought it sounded an odd sort of job to be doing but it turned out to be confidential book writer for all the ships.

The WRNS uniform might have been attractive but to Barbara Jones there were certain garments that were somewhat less than desirable.

BARBARA JONES

You went into what they called the 'slops' – that was the stores. And the WRNS behind the counter would look at you and slap down a jacket and then a skirt. Two of each and a bit of everything. Then I saw what they called 'blackouts', these huge bloomers with long legs. They were hideous. We said, 'We don't have to wear these, do we?' They said, 'No, don't worry about them. You just put them out for kit inspection.'

Barbara Jones, WRNS rating, taken January 1945.

Sometimes the ways of service life were strange and well beyond the experience of Welsh girls who were living away from home, most of them for the first time in their lives.

MARY PHILLIPS

One Christmas Day in the Mess, all the officers kept inviting us to have a drink with them. Well, in those days I didn't drink. The only alcoholic drinks I'd ever heard of were port and sherry. So that's what I had. Every time I served one of them I had to have a tot for myself. I was so ill. I felt awful – I think I was sick for days afterwards.

BARBARA JONES

When we were training there was a girl, the same age as me, in the bunk above. We could hear this drone and I was trying to work out if it was a British or German plane. Then somebody in the dormitory said, 'It's a buzz bomb.' We listened to it, then the engine cut out. It seemed to go on forever, that silence. And then we heard a huge explosion. We breathed a sigh of relief because it wasn't us who'd got it.

Then I realised that the bunk above was shaking. I asked the girl if she was all right. 'No, no,' she said. She was really upset because she'd never been in a raid before. I said, 'You can come in with me if you're frightened.' I'd always slept with one of my sisters so it was nothing to me.

In the morning there was somebody shaking the foot of the bunk – a Petty Officer. 'What's this?' I told her that the girl was frightened because of the buzz bombs. She said, 'Don't you know it's an offence to have two in a bed?' At the time I thought it was because you might breathe germs over the person next to you – we'd had lectures on hygiene, head lice and things like that. I thought that if one or the other of us had a cold or head lice we'd pass them across. And it wasn't until after the war that I realised the real reason. That's how green we were.

Working in the Officers' Mess meant that, sometimes, VIPs had to be entertained or looked after.

MARY PHILLIPS

We had lots of pilots passing through. They'd land, eat a meal and be gone. The one person I remember, really remember, was Lord Gort. We were told he was coming in one morning, on his way to some meeting or other. We had to be in our best bib and tucker – but he hardly noticed. He was very polite but, really, he just ate his breakfast and took off again.

WAAF training at Morecambe. Mary Phillips stands second from the right in the middle row.

BARBARA JONES

On our afternoons off we'd go to Llanystumdwy and throw stones into the river. Sometimes this rather short man with grey hair – long, but very thin – he'd chat with us, ask us where we were from and what not. He used to wear a black trilby and a black cape – it had seen better days, that cape. But that was that, he was our little old gentleman.

Then we heard that Lloyd George had died. All the photographs were in the paper and we thought, 'Oh, gosh, that's our little old gentleman.' Those of us who used to talk to him went to the funeral. It was a very simple funeral. The coffin came up on a farm cart, pulled by an old dray horse. It had trails of leaves coming right over the cart, coming down over the coffin. I remember the colours because on the other side of the river there were two fields and it was a mass of colour. People were singing hymns. It was absolutely gorgeous.

There were compensations for being away from home in the services. And some of them, in those days of wartime austerity, were greatly appreciated by the folks back home.

MARY PHILLIPS

One of the aircrews, they'd got hold of some bananas. Well, you never saw a banana in those days, they were really rare. They gave me one and the next time I went home I took it with me. Everyone was thrilled. We spent hours just looking at it.

DENISE LLEWELLYN

The American soldiers were passing through the docks and the girls would all go home with, perhaps, sixty packets of cigarettes each – Camel and Lucky Strike, I seem to remember. I didn't smoke but my father was quite a heavy smoker. I just commented about this one day and he said, 'Well, why don't you bring home sixty packets of cigarettes for me?' And I said, 'I wouldn't like to take them because I don't smoke.' And he said, 'I think you'd better start smoking right away, my girl.'

Mary Phillips in WAAF uniform at Talbenny aerodrome.

The Second World War undoubtedly changed women's lives for ever, not just because it gave them the opportunity to earn money but also because of the wide

range of experiences they enjoyed – or endured. After 1945, expectations were
different. It was a brave new world and women were not going to go back to the
same old routines they had kept before the war.

BARBARA JONES

The men were given a demob suit but the women were just given clothing
coupons because, I suppose, not every woman wanted to wear the same suit.
You had your gratuity book – so much of your pay was put away for you
during the war and given to you at the end. So you came out with some money.
I think I had twenty pounds – which was a lot of money in those days.

The doctor put a stethoscope on your chest and patted you on the back. The
dentist counted your teeth. And that was it. You were out.

'I don't think I'd ever heard of a Scouse person or a Geordie until I joined
up. Then, suddenly, all these different accents all around you. A lot of
people didn't know my accent. I'd be asked what part of Scotland I came
from. Or Ireland – was I north or south?

Barbara Jones, WRNS

# Chapter Seven

# Children at War

Children, perhaps more than any other section of Britain's society, should have been aware of the preparations for war during the late 1930s. Comics, newsreel features at the cinema and, above all, cigarette cards continually pumped out a diet of war, aggression and what was likely to come. One of the most popular cigarette-card collections in those final few years before 1939 was the WD and HO Wills set entitled 'Air Raid Precautions'. In graphic pictures it showed people how to deal with incendiary bombs, how to build gas-proof shelters and how to fit their gas masks.

And yet children, like everybody else, did not believe war would really come. After all, surely nobody would repeat the madness of 1914-18? Besides, there were more important things to do or think about than Hitler and his funny, goose-stepping followers. For those children who did concern themselves with war it was invariably the glamour and the appeal of soldiers and battles – fuelled by the Hollywood vision of conflict – that was foremost in their minds.

So when the war erupted in September 1939, children, like everyone else, were caught totally by surprise. Children are resilient, however, and quickly euphoria and adventure took hold, as WARWICK TAYLOR and HARRY HIGHMAN remember.

WARWICK TAYLOR

> I was 13 years of age at the time and I was still at school of course. As a young teenager, I found it all very exciting. They were exciting times. It was an adventure really because no-one knew what was going to happen.

HARRY HIGHMAN

> Oh, it was wonderful – you know, gosh, we were going to hear guns firing. We were all excited, it was going to be marvellous. As children we always played at war. We had an old rifle and a tin helmet. We were always running around the fields, before the war started, always playing soldiers. So the war, for us children, was something to look forward to. You see, I suppose a lot of the old First War soldiers didn't tell us much about their war. We just didn't realise.

Playing, particularly in those days when childhood seemed to last a lot, lot longer, was always important – and continued to be so, right through the war years, even though the games and interests changed slightly. BILL HARRIES and SYLVIE BAILEY remember some of the games they played.

BILL HARRIES

> We didn't have all they've got today. We didn't even have balls and things. One game, you threw a lump of wood up in the air and whoever it fell on, he had to chase us around with that lump of wood. That's the type of thing we did. Just chucking a lump of wood at one another – a small piece, not really hurtful.

SYLVIE BAILEY

> We had hopscotch and rounders, marbles and 'Mob'. For 'Mob', you shut your eyes, counted to twenty and then you had to find your friends. Indoors, at night, we played games like Snakes and Ladders or Ludo and Snap. Lots of the games have come down the generations and are still played today.
>
> We got around by bus or by bicycle. Or simply by walking. There was no being picked up by cars. Very few people had cars during the war years as petrol was rationed. But only rich people had cars anyway. Once a year you might have a real treat – to go by train to Barry Island for the day.

To begin with, dyecast or model toys continued to be available. Many of the pre-war toys, particularly high quality ones, had been made in Germany by firms like Bing. Once hostilities began such products were no longer available but British manufacturers soon filled the void, producing a wide range of military toys, items such as aeroplanes, warships and tanks. As the war dragged on, however, raw materials became a problem and toys were in very short supply.

For many children, it was simply a case of making do with toys that had been purchased before the war. And, often, these items were already channelling youngsters in the direction of particular employment.

HARRY HIGHMAN

> My interest in mechanical items had begun before the war when I was about eight years old. I was lucky enough to have access to a Meccano construction set which belonged to my brother Cyril. He was five years older than me but had little interest in this construction toy. It consisted of items of pierced steel strips, angle irons, plates, wheels and brackets. They could be assembled and bolted together into shapes and designs – the only limiting factor being the number of bits in your Meccano set. Whenever I had any spare pocket money, which was not often – or maybe I'd swap bits with my friends – I'd get some more items to add to my stock of Meccano.
>
> I spent hours constructing things like cranes, lorries and bridges. It taught me a lot about engineering and design and I developed an active interest in all aspects of mechanical functions, including repairing or adjusting anything mechanical – especially bicycles and sewing machines.

One of the new crazes that developed as the war progressed was the curious hobby of collecting shrapnel. It was a pastime that was followed by both boys and girls.

BARBARA JONES

We'd go out and look for shrapnel. I used to save it for my younger half-sister. She had a tin full of old bits of shrapnel. We used to see who could find the biggest piece. Most of it, I think, was from anti-aircraft guns. Maybe some was from bombs but most, I think, was from the guns

CYRIL ACTIE and TERRY POWELL remember their shrapnel-collecting escapades with glee.

CYRIL ACTIE

After a raid, next morning, we'd all go collecting shrapnel – you know, the odd pieces of bombs. There was always a lot of noise during a raid, ack-ack going off even if the planes were going over, as they did sometimes, going to attack somewhere else.

TERRY POWELL

I can remember going round the streets collecting shrapnel from the shells – anti-aircraft shells, probably. I can remember going to look at the bomb craters – as children do. Just to see what was there.

You'd go out in the morning, looking for shrapnel and there was always plenty of it in the streets after a raid. We also used to find incendiary bombs that had been dropped. I remember collecting all this stuff and taking it back home. My father was most annoyed because I'd brought these incendiary bombs back home.

He was a warden on the docks, an air-raid warden. He was heavily involved with protection against fire – you shouldn't touch these things, he'd say. But as a child you collected it. Everybody had great collections of shrapnel and you compared yours with your friends.

"AIR DEFENCE" DISPLAY by Territorial Army Units

Anti-aircraft battery

Many schools in Britain were closed for a week following the declaration of war but they were soon open again and children found themselves back in the old routine. Once the bombing began in earnest, however, changes began to make themselves felt.

Many teachers had enlisted in the forces and their replacements were sometimes pulled out of retirement. Some school buildings were requisitioned as fire stations or as ambulance stations, while others were destroyed in bombing raids. It meant that schools often had to find emergency accommodation and, sometimes, this was far from adequate.

ALAN WORRELL

>The school I used to go to, Moorland Road School, was bombed out, completely devastated. So I spent most of my school days in what's termed as East Moors Hall. There were quite a few classes there, all lumped into the one big room, so the education we received wasn't exactly bright. You'd have a teacher talking at one end of the room and another teacher talking at the other – noise everywhere.

BILL HARRIES

>We used to go to school in the Defensible Barracks just outside the town. It was an old barrack block for soldiers – and we shared our school with them. It was a big old Victorian building – very cold in winter.

CYRIL ACTIE

>I hated school. I was always the bad one because, well they can say what they like, but I believe it was part racialism. We had all sorts in there and the teachers didn't seem to like that much. I was left-handed as well. They used to beat me for being left-handed. I never really learned anything. I left school at fourteen and most of what I learned I learned after I left school.

SYLVIE BAILEY

>The discipline, oh, it was very strict. If you dared to answer the teachers back you'd be sent to the Head to have the cane. The subjects were more or less the same as today – the 3Rs, history and geography. And you had cookery and laundry – you were taught how to wash clothes in a boiler, with a scrubbing board and then iron them. You had marks out of ten for it!
>
>Our school had a little flat where you learned how to clean a house, to make beds and lay the table properly. It was called Housewifery. I passed the exam for the Grammar School but I couldn't go as my father had been killed early on in the war and my mum was poor. We just didn't have the £5 for the uniform.

CYRIL ACTIE

>The school day was basically the same as before the war. We had to be there by nine and stayed till 12.00. Then 2.00 till half past four. It wasn't a great school – the only thing I did well at was arithmetic. Nobody could beat me at figures. But as for reading and writing, they never taught me much.
>
>We had one teacher, he came there before I finished, and he told my mother that the trouble was, I didn't want to learn. That was true – all I ever did was fight the teachers. That was all I ever wanted to do, he said.

It was hard to keep children on target when lessons might be disrupted any minute by air-raid sirens or bombs. And if there was tragedy – as in the case of Cwmparc, just outside Treorchy – then it invariably affected the whole community. The Log Book for Cwmparc Junior School bleakly but accurately records the affect of the air raid in April 1941 when 27 people were killed in the village.

> The school was closed after an air raid on Cwmparc the previous night. Three pupils lost their lives. Many inhabitants are now homeless.

Cwmparc School re-opened the following day, when 70 children were present. Such bold facts do not even begin to describe the trauma that many children endured during these years. And yet it was a trauma that they often seemed to take in their stride.

BILL HARRIES

> I was three or four years old when war broke out. My mother used to look after all the small children in the street. When the siren went she'd take us down to the woods and we'd play there happily. We used to enjoy that. Particularly when we could see the planes. We didn't know what destruction they were doing. We used to like seeing them go over. Mother used to shout at us, 'Get back into the trees.' When it was all over we used to come back up from the woods.

Once, however, what Bill Harries and his mother came back to was not exactly what they had expected.

BILL HARRIES

> This particular day, with all the noise and banging and things going off, we were frightened, us kids, we were very frightened. We saw plumes of black smoke and as we went back home afterwards there were slates and timber and stones all over the street.
>
> When we got to our house half of it had gone. All the houses below us were completely demolished. At our back door, Mother asked me to give her a hand. She couldn't open it on her own. I was pushing at the back door and when I got it open there was about fifteen inches of black flake from the fire.
>
> I'll always remember the RAF coming along and putting up a tin partition. We lived in the rest of the house, the bit that was left behind this tin partition, for the rest of the war.

Bombing raids, shrapnel-collecting, aeroplanes flying overhead – the war years were certainly different for children. Right from the beginning one of the many new experiences they were faced with was wearing evil-smelling gas masks.

Poison gas had been used during the First World War, to devastating effect. The fear of a mass gas attack remained in the minds of politicians and ex-soldiers alike and, consequently, successive governments built up a huge supply of protective gas masks. During the Munich Crisis a large number of these were issued to the general public and, by the outbreak of the war, only babies and small children had not been given gas masks. Babies and small children required special equipment – a gas hood (or baby bag as it was called) for babies and the special Small Child's Respirator for children. These became available as 1939 wore on. Almost immediately, the Small Child's Respirator became known as the Mickey Mouse Gas Mask.

PATTI FLYNN

I remember my Mickey Mouse Gas Mask. Most gas masks were made out of black rubber. But for the little ones, us children, they made them in red with a black nose – just like Mickey Mouse, so that children wouldn't be afraid when they were put into them.

Official wisdom advised that children should wear their masks as often as possible. Otherwise, it was felt, when a gas attack was launched they would be too frightened to get the masks on in time. In reality, children soon became accustomed to the masks, as BRYAN HOPE recalls.

BRYAN HOPE

The gas mask had a single eyepiece that stuck into this thin rubber mask and a snout, very much like a pig's snout, I suppose. We used to have to carry these with us in little cardboard boxes, hanging from a piece of string on our shoulder.

We used to take these to school and every now and again the teacher would call out 'Gas', in which case we had to get our masks out and put them on. We soon realised that by blocking the intake, the end of the snout as it were, and then blowing, air was expelled from the sides of the mask. And very realistic farting sounds were made. Of course you'd hear the muffled laughter from inside the gas mask. The teachers got a bit fed up of this.

Sometimes, carrying gas masks was a nuisance. At other times, however, the cardboard cases were useful as goalposts or wickets for games of street soccer and cricket. And sometimes the masks themselves were used in games as BOB EVANS remembers.

Cigarette card showing how to fit and remove gas masks.

BOB EVANS

> They had a filter on the end which contained some charcoal or something which filtered out gasses. But once they were discarded we used to use these for kicking about. 1940 was a most awful winter. You could almost freeze a hot-water bottle in the bed. The canal was at the bottom of the hill. We used to play ice hockey there, using the bottom end of the gas mask as a puck and a stick pulled out of the hedge.

Children had belonged to clubs and organisations like the Boy Scouts or Girl Guides for years. During the war, these youth groups quickly fine-tuned their activities in order to help children and young people to 'do their bit'. Collecting metal salvage or helping in hospitals were just two of the jobs they carried out.

The Boy Scouts were soon offering a Civil Defence Badge as part of their training while their Scout War Service Badge included tasks like signalling, first aid and unarmed combat. Many scouts took on jobs like building or erecting Morrison Shelters while others – the more experienced of them – were actually used to help train the Home Guard in field craft. Girl Guides carried out work in first-aid posts and sometimes helped to distribute children's gas masks.

For many young people, however, the more military organisations held a greater appeal. The Air Training Corps was established in 1941 with the intention of providing early training for boys who would later enlist in the Royal Air Force. Many schools quickly established their own ATC Squadron, where young boys would drill, work on aircraft identification and, sometimes, even get to fly.

WARWICK TAYLOR, who is now the President of the Bevin Boys Association, remembers the atmosphere well.

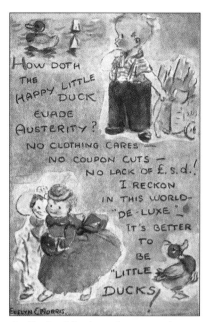

An Evelyn Morris card, commenting on the days of austerity.

Children, like adults, were affected by rationing.

WARWICK TAYLOR

I'd actually left school and started work as a junior clerk – for the grand salary of £78 per annum. I was still in the Air Training Corps, however. Most of us were in those days. Most youngsters of my age, we were all in some form of cadet corps – army, navy or air force cadets – and I was in the Air Training Corps. By the time I left school I'd already completed three and a half years' service. The plan, of course, was to go into the Royal Air Force when I was called up.

HARRY HIGHMAN

In 1942, I joined the Air Training Corps in Newport, as a cadet. It was a wonderful experience for me – and others – because we visited so many RAF Stations. We went on annual camp which cost us, I think, only about twelve shillings – and that was just for our food.

You had so many opportunities to fly in planes as a passenger. If you were lucky you could fly in a Tiger Moth or an Anson, a Dragon Rapide or even a Lancaster.

You stood at the end of the runway and you sort of scrounged your way in. You said to the pilot, 'Can I carry your chute, sir?' And he'd say, 'You want to fly? Get in, then.' You had to have your own chute as well – what would have happened if anything went wrong, I don't know. You sat on the floor, tucked away in the corner. It wasn't an operational flight, of course. Just on training flights.

For Harry Highman, it wasn't just the annual camp that had such a huge appeal. Living in south Wales, he had easy access to a large number of RAF bases.

HARRY HIGHMAN

I visited lots of different camps – Pembrey in west Wales, Cosford in the Midlands, St Athan in the Vale of Glamorgan. At St Athan there was a gliding school. We were all encouraged to go gliding and learn how to fly gliders. We'd usually go down to St Athan on a Saturday and do a bit of gliding that day. We'd stay overnight, on the camp, and do the same thing

Harry Highman (left) as an ATC cadet at Barry Island. The other boy is Ralph Hughes.

on the Sunday before we travelled back home. For our entertainment on the Saturday night, we'd go into Barry Island or places like that. And I suppose we'd do what all youngsters did in the evenings in those days.

Girls, too, sometimes enjoyed military discipline and activity. BARBARA JONES vividly remembers her time in the Girl's Training Corps.

BARBARA JONES

> You all had to do your bit, even down to giving your saucepans away. Whatever you did, you thought you were really helping to win the war and I joined the Girls' Training Corps. I really enjoyed that.
>
> We used to go to the Infirmary and help out on the wards. Sometimes we used to do washing-up. Then, another time, we had a load of old gas-mask containers and we had to cut off all the metal parts for salvage. That was hard work, very tough. We did lots of other things as well, things like learning morse code and practising aircraft identification.
>
> It was always there, in the back of your mind, that we were doing our bit to win the war. We knew we were going to win, all the girls did. I didn't ever think we wouldn't.

Sometimes, young boys did more than simply join a voluntary organisation – sometimes they chose a path that would give them a head start in their future career. For GEORGE BLAKE and RAY NEWBERRY that meant careers at sea.

GEORGE BLAKE

> I went to a school that was for boys who were intending to go into the Mercantile Marine. Lady Furness, the wife of MP Christopher Furness – he was a ship owner – subscribed to or started our school. We had a sort of semi-naval uniform and most of the boys were sons of either Royal Naval or Merchant Navy personnel.

RAY NEWBERRY

> I went to a pre-school training establishment – HMS *Worcester*. The school used to be an old wooden warship moored out in the Thames off Greenhithe but, during the war, she was being used as a mother craft for the Thames Patrol of the Royal Navy. As a result we were kicked out, as it were, and lived ashore in Kent. We did retain the old *Cutty Sark*, which was moored alongside the *Worcester*, and we used to go down there for our seamanship training.

For most young people, however, school was usually just a building at the end of the road and the subjects no more interesting than the usual English and Maths of the time. Only in the evenings and at weekends did they really come alive.

Young boys like Harry Highman spent a lot of their formative years in organisations such as the ATC. He rose to the rank of Flight Sergeant before, at the age of 21, becoming the civilian adjutant of his squadron. In particular, he remembers being part of the Victory Parade in London at the end of the war.

HARRY HIGHMAN

I was lucky, at the end of the war, when I was one of four cadets to go to the Victory Parade in London. Four cadets from every squadron of the ATC were picked out to take part.

We went up to London and were billeted up there in Camden Town Deep Underground station – which was way down below the normal station. There were about 5000 cadets there. You can imagine what it was like, walking along this tube-like area to your bunk.

And then, the following day, we went out on training parades. I can remember walking down the Mall with all the crowds and everything. It's something I'll never forget.

With death and destruction ever looming it seemed almost natural that romance should blossom or bloom for young adults, barely out of their adolescence. Many married couples met for the first time during the war.

MARY PHILLIPS

I met my husband, as he later became, in 1940. He'd come back from Dunkirk earlier in the year and was with a radar unit at West Pennar, about seven or eight miles away. His friend was distantly related to us and suggested they visit. They walked all eight miles, through deep snow, to Pembroke. When they got to our front door my father took one look at the pair, listened to their

Mary Phillips's wedding day – husband and wife just out of the forces.

thick Scottish and North Country accents and chased them down the road with a pitchfork. He thought they were German spies! They came back later and Jack and I were married after the war.

DORIS CURTIS

I met my husband when I was still in the Land Army. He'd come out of the army and was working for the WARAG as a mechanic. So I never went back home. We got married, I came out of the Land Army and settled in Carmarthen.

SYLVIE BAILEY

It was all very strict in those days, growing up during the war. When you were older you could go courting, with your boyfriend, in the back row of the cinema – the same cinema where we used to go to watch cartoons and films on a Saturday morning when we were young. If you were lucky, you could sometimes have your boyfriend in the parlour for the evening, for a bit of a cuddle. But your mum and dad would always shout 'Time' at about 10.00 pm.

Lasting memories from those war years also stay with evacuees – memories both good and bad. The government had set out its plans for wholesale evacuation long before war began. The air raids of the First World War, limited as they may have been, had alerted people to the danger of attack from the air and children, the most vulnerable group in society, it was reasoned, would be better off out of the target areas should conflict arrive.

Accordingly, the country was divided into three sections – neutral, reception and evacuation. Neutral areas were parts where there was not considered to be any great danger. Reception areas were the safest part of Britain where evacuees could be housed. And evacuation areas, of course, were those places or parts of the country where there was a very real danger of death and destruction from enemy bombs.

The order to begin evacuating children was given on 31st August, 1939, three days before war broke out. Over the following week, two million people, most of them children, were sent out of the cities and industrial towns into the countryside.

Wales was quickly identified as one of the main reception areas, while big cities like London, Birmingham and Liverpool were clearly part of the evacuation areas. The process was logical: schools were evacuated en masse, teachers moving with their pupils to rural parts of the country. Children from the same families were to be kept together and very young children were evacuated with their mothers. In reality, however, things were never that simple – or as caring. DENNIS BARRATT was evacuated from London, NORMA WAGNER from Liverpool, and both of them remember the process only too well.

DENNIS BARRATT

As a seven-year-old, more or less an infant, I remember a crocodile of little ones having to walk to school. There we were tagged with a luggage label with our name and details about us. And then we were taken by bus to a station and put on a train.

NORMA WAGNER

> We missed the tram and so my mother flagged down a bread van. And he gave us a lift to Lime Street Station. When we got there I remember seeing rows and rows of children. I had a label on my cardigan and there were rows of children with their gas masks and labels on their blazers and jackets and that.
>
> I don't remember my mother saying goodbye or anything. I just remember the teacher that was with us filing us onto the train. And that was it.

Although, at the time of the Munich Crisis, almost 80% of London's parents had declared that they wished their children to be evacuated, in 1939 only half of them took advantage of the scheme. Even so, London buses still carried 230,000 evacuees to the main-line railway stations and, on some parts of the Thames, evacuation was actually carried out by boat.

The evacuation of children from the large cities was incredibly efficient and well-handled. In the reception areas, however, things were much less successful. Children were pushed around from one place to another in an attempt to find suitable lodgings and, most crucial of all, families were often broken up. It meant that, inevitably, a large number of youngsters would soon start to drift back home into the danger areas.

For VIOLET CROPPER, the problem of younger sisters to take care of was always at the forefront of her mind – and when her mum and dad were suddenly not around, that was a very real responsibility.

VIOLET CROPPER

> We got on the train and Mum and Dad were very upset. They asked me to look after the two other children, my sisters. Mum said, 'Try and stay together. Please stay together.'
>
> On the train young Jean was sick. She didn't remember much about it – she was just a baby, really. And Esther wasn't happy, either. We were all really emotional. But, being the eldest, I was thinking, 'Where are we going? When are we going to get there?'

When the evacuees arrived at their destinations, they were still not through their ordeal. North Wales was an ideal reception area for English children, particularly from cities like Liverpool and Manchester, and for Welsh youngsters like ELUNED GILES, living in a village outside Caernarfon, the new arrivals were almost exotic in their appeal.

ELUNED GILES

> Us Welsh children in Llanllyfni, we'd never been further than Bangor or Pwllheli. Evacuees were something alien as far as we were concerned. Anyway, the day came and they told us in school that the evacuees were arriving by train at Penygroes station.
>
> So, of course, we all got together and off we went to Penygroes to wait for this train to come in. Well, the train was packed with children, some of them

with carrier bags, some with little suitcases, others with just a comic. Holding hands, some of them, with their name tags on their chests, and crying.

They came to Llanllyfni school and we all trooped in after them. People were standing there, picking the children out – 'I'll have him.' Or 'I'll have her.' Or 'There's two of them, sisters – oh, I won't take two of them, I'll only take one.'

## VIOLET CROPPER

Someone said we were going to a place where there was a beach. Well, being from a family of nine, I thought 'Beach? That will be nice.' I tried to comfort the others with that.

## DENNIS BARRATT

We had this long, long train journey and I suddenly found myself in this tiny village in mid Wales. In the village there were no mains services of any kind, no electricity, no laid-on water, nothing of that nature. And the first night I began to wonder, 'How am I going to survive this?'

## VIOLET CROPPER

We were lined up and people were there to choose the children they were going to take in. And as the line was getting shorter, I said to myself, 'What's happening?' I was afraid Jean was going to be sick again and I thought, 'Nobody's going to take us.'

A man came up – he only had one arm – and he lifted up my sister Jean and said, 'Come along with me, children.' And off we went and we arrived at the Roberts'.

In Machynlleth, DELYTH REES had been looking forward to the arrival of the evacuees – after all, it meant someone to play with. BET ROWLANDS of Trefenter near Aberystwyth felt the same. And yet things did not quite turn out the way they expected.

## DELYTH REES

We were allocated a little girl about the same age as myself. But unfortunately she was very, very homesick. She couldn't speak Welsh and I didn't have much English, so we couldn't talk very well.

I remember her sitting on the stairs, crying, wanting to go home. And me trying to give her my teddy bear to play with. But she wouldn't have him, she didn't want anything.

## BET ROWLANDS

It caused quite an uproar, quite an upheaval, because it was something unusual in our small community. A bus load of English children coming over? It was unusual, you know.

My Aunty May went down to get an evacuee. She chose one, a pretty girl with red cheeks. They said she couldn't have her because she was one of sisters. But there was a little one there, without a brother or sister. And that was Norma. She was standing at the back, quite alone.

NORMA WAGNER

I was taken out from behind the desk. The woman took my hand and Bet joined us somewhere in the yard. And I was taken up the lane, holding their hands.

Norma Wagner might have been apprehensive on the journey to Machynlleth – what she now felt was pure terror.

NORMA WAGNER

It was at this point that I got rather afraid of what was happening to me. There was this droning speech going on each side of me. It was a very strange language and quite frightening.

Hearing people speaking in Welsh was only the start of it. Soon things became even worse.

NORMA WAGNER

When I walked into the house, I saw this big cauldron on the fire. Well, I really thought they were witches.

I remember crying a lot and feeling quite ill. My eyes were very sore and puffy.

After four days, however, Norma stopped crying and refusing to eat. Soon she was out in the fields, playing happily and collecting buttercups.

BET ROWLANDS

I thought to myself, 'I hope this little girl's going to speak to me better than this' – I'd been looking forward to having this evacuee. Well, in no time, she didn't let us down. She was talking away and we were doing all sorts of things together.

Dennis Barratt was sent away from London for the second time in 1944, when the V2 rockets were being launched against the city in a last dramatic attempt to bring Britain to her knees. Even at that late stage in the war, Wales was felt to be far safer than the south of England.

DENNIS BARRATT

I was billeted with a bachelor chap who was the local postmaster. He ran not only the post office, but also a little general store. He had what you could call a cook/housekeeper although she was always referred to as the Maid. School happened to be next door to where I was billeted. So I'd get up in the mornings

– of course, washing facilities were a pitcher and a basin of cold water in the room – and come down to breakfast ready laid out and then, off next door to school. Back at lunchtime for a good meal and, of course, it was wartime still; it was incredible. After school the time was entirely mine to go out with my new friends. They started to teach me some words of Welsh. The first few words were fine. They taught me the usual things – 'Nos da', 'Bora da', 'Diolch.' But then they also taught me a few other words, words I should never have been taught. They told me to practise them on the village curate.

Teaching evacuees a few swear words was mild compared to some of the goings-on.

ELUNED GILES

We were Welsh – they couldn't understand us and we couldn't understand them. Of course, like children everywhere, we took an instant dislike to one another. It changed later on, mind you. But not then.

We understood some words they used – 'Daft', we knew that, knew that it was bad. So that meant we had to have a battle, the whole of Llanllyfni children against the evacuees, by the bridge down at the bottom of the village.

We were to meet them there, each side of the bridge. And, of course, the weapons we collected before we went down – stones, sticks, all sorts. Oh, what we were going to do to them, you know! They'd have been better off facing the Germans!

Anyway, when we got there, there was nobody there at all. The teachers had got to know what was going on and they'd taken them off around the countryside, to see the animals and so on.

Sometimes, for reasons beyond the control of the authorities or the children, evacuees had to be moved. That was fine if they were going to a better situation but occasionally, as in the case of Violet Cropper and her sisters, it meant a much more unpleasant experience.

VIOLET CROPPER

After, I think, about twelve months, we were moved. We went to Queen Street, which was a horrible billet. We had porridge with no sugar on and we were put in the outhouse to get washed in cold water.

And then, on a Sunday, it was, 'Come on, get up, you've got to go out now. Go to the station and wait for the Liverpool bus.' That was a special bus which the parents or sisters and brothers were allowed to come on to visit the children. If Mum or Dad or our sisters weren't on it, there'd be a little parcel of apples and oranges, nothing very much, just a few sweets and things.

The evacuee children might have been protected, out in the Welsh countryside, but the bombing of Britain's industrial heartlands often brought tragedy to the separated families. Violet Cropper remembers it well.

VIOLET CROPPER

> We'd be there, waiting, and the bus would come. And sometimes people would get off that bus and take the children to one side, to tell them that their parents had been killed in the air raids. And that they wouldn't be coming any more. It was so sad, it really was.

The evacuation of children undoubtedly caused pain and suffering for many, although it probably saved quite a number of lives as well. Ultimately, the system was doomed to failure because it separated children from their loved ones at a time of great national crisis. From the beginning, therefore, there was a steady stream of evacuees returning to the cities. By the middle of October 1939, almost 50,000 mothers and children had returned to London alone and in November of the same year the number of returning children was so great that schools in the evacuation areas were having to re-open. By the spring of 1940, it was estimated that 400,000 children were still living in the capital.

For some, the memory of evacuation and all that it entailed remains vivid and painful – both for the English children who were evacuated and for the Welsh youngsters who welcomed them into their homes.

ELUNED GILES

> When I think of it now, you know, it was all so hard. The little things – they were only about five or seven – and all holding hands and crying. It must have been terrible for their parents.

VIOLET CROPPER

> We did get used to it in the end but the day couldn't come quickly enough for us to return to our parents.

---

'We were frightened to death of the evacuees coming down; we were wondering if we'd have to go away as well. It was frightening for children at that time. But when they came the evacuees were well received, on the whole. Being a friendly community we accepted them as relations, more than anything, and they quickly settled down into school.'

Mary Evans, Cwmparc

# Chapter Eight

# Fighting Differently

Many people in Wales fought their war in somewhat different or unusual fashions. Conscientious objectors, for example, felt that they could not take up arms against their fellow human beings and therefore lodged their protests in the only way they knew how – by refusing to fight. All conscientious objectors were called in front of Tribunals where their cases were duly judged. And yet, even in these supposedly neutral hearings, individual pacifists encountered vastly different responses, as SHEILA and BARRIE NAYLOR and JOHN CLEDAN MEARS can testify.

JOHN CLEDAN MEARS

My initial reaction when war broke out was, well, so many of my contemporaries and friends are being conscripted, they're going to the front: what am I going to do about it? How do I reconcile this with what I believe as a Christian, with what I know about the teachings of Jesus Christ? I couldn't possibly reconcile the two in my mind. I was in a real dilemma.

What I did was read the Gospels and look at what Jesus did and taught. I talked it over with some of my seniors. I remember one particular person, a schoolmaster. He was a profound thinker and we used to be up until the early hours of the morning. He used to challenge me with questions I found difficult to understand. But it helped to clarify my position.

In the end I came down to this – how in the name of Christ could I go out and kill somebody? I couldn't.

BARRIE NAYLOR

I was a pacifist from early on. I was teaching at Sibford School near Banbury. It was a Quaker school and all of the staff there were pacifists. We cultivated our ideas quite a lot at Sibford before the war.

Pacifism means a respect for life which doesn't allow you to enter war and kill your

Barrie Naylor (left) with Sir Stafford Cripps.

fellow human beings. The chief aim of pacifism is to create a life which will prevent the killing of humans. I wasn't a Quaker but I became one while I was at Sibford. The influence of the other teachers – and the children – made me convert to Quakerism.

SHEILA NAYLOR

Like Barrie, I wasn't a Quaker before I went to Sibford. I had leanings before, though. My grandfather, on my mother's side, was German. He had settled in Britain, married my grandmother and had a very tough time during the First World War. So I'd been aware of the difficulties caused by war in that respect. I had German relatives and I just felt that it wasn't possible for me to be able to support a war of that kind again. And then I became a Quaker at Sibford.

BARRIE NAYLOR

It was a question of talking to your fellow Quakers and deciding what you were going to do. You had to decide, when asked to attend a Tribunal, what you would say, what you would accept. Tribunals would offer you this, that, the other. Sometimes it would be work on the land, sometimes you'd go to prison, sometimes you were allowed to carry on what you were doing.

SHEILA NAYLOR

You just had to accept what might be offered or what you were condemned to. That is the whole basis of Quakerism. You have to do what you think is right, regardless.

JOHN CLEDAN MEARS

You heard of people within the German regime standing up in the way that I was endeavouring to do. You heard later about people who resisted to the end and lost their lives. Would I be prepared to do that? That was my intention. Whether I could carry it out – that would be the question.

Barrie Naylor and John Cledan Mears were called to Tribunals early on in the war. Cledan Mears was a student of theology – later he went on to become Bishop of Bangor but, at the time, he was just seventeen years old.

JOHN CLEDAN MEARS

I went to the Tribunal – the Local Tribunal as they called it. It was held in Aberystwyth and there were three people on the bench, one of them the Chairman. They asked very challenging questions, rightly so. But it was very confrontational. 'Intimidating' is another word I could use.

These three men on the bench, they were exchanging whispers behind each other's backs and laughing and winking and so on. Then they'd put questions straight at you. 'How can you justify your stance when Jesus himself used force?' they asked. 'Do you know that story?' I said, 'Yes, the cleansing of the Temple. It's in the four Gospels.' So they asked what chapter and verse. Well, I wasn't that acquainted with the story so I wasn't able to answer. To my surprise and amusement the headline in *The Western Mail* next morning was 'Theological Student Doesn't Know His Bible!'

BARRIE NAYLOR

I went to a Tribunal near Banbury, I think. There was no hostility, it was just that they were doing their job and I was trying to help them. They decided that I should do agricultural work. But I didn't want to do that. It would have meant putting another man out of work and then he'd have to go and fight. So, in the end, I refused.

SHEILA NAYLOR

Barrie was called to another Tribunal at Oxford. The bombing of London had started and they were a bit more hostile that time. He asked to be allowed to do social work and, at the time, the Quakers were very busy, getting all kinds of things going. He was told there was a need for somebody in the Rhondda, doing work with the Boys' Clubs which had been started. And so he was sent down to Trealaw.

I didn't have to go in front of a Tribunal. I just carried on teaching for a term and then I went to join Barrie in the Rhondda.

JOHN CLEDAN MEARS

Another question the Tribunal asked was, 'Do you realise that your contemporaries are risking their lives crossing the Atlantic, facing the U-boats, to bring food to this country so that the likes of you can exist?' I said, 'I realise that. I appreciate my debt to them. But what is the alternative? If I don't eat I have to commit suicide.' And their retort was, 'Well, that's what you should do.'

Barrie and Sheila Naylor were married in 1940, just before they came to Wales and were more than a little surprised at the reaction of people in the Rhondda Valley to the conscientious objectors who had suddenly arrived in their midst.

SHEILA NAYLOR

It was quite remarkable really. We expected hostility and, in a way, deserved it. But people were remarkably tolerant, especially in the Rhondda,

The Settlement where we were based in Trealaw had done such wonderful work that they accepted us, as Quakers, coming in. We would be the same – no problem. There was relief that they had work there again after so many years of depression; the men were working. And a lot of the women, too. There was no sort of jingoism there. That's what struck us.

BARRIE NAYLOR

The Rhondda people were tolerant. They understood, if I may put it like that. We were accepted without any trouble at all. It was amazing to me but they accepted us. It's natural for people who want to fight and kill to object to those who don't. We understood that and would have accepted it. We expected it but we didn't get it.

John Cledan Mears, however, was not so lucky. His experience at the Tribunal was reflected in the way that people, generally, looked at him once he had declared himself a conscientious objector. He did not resent it but knew, like all people of conscience, that he had to do what was right. Nevertheless, he was still troubled by his decision.

JOHN CLEDAN MEARS

> I had already heard that my cousin in the RAF had been brought down. When, a bit later, some of my colleagues came to grief in the front line it was very distressing indeed. I began to ask myself, 'Am I a coward in not being prepared to do what they have done?'
>
> The general reaction was, here is a young man not prepared to do what most others do, risk his life. I well remember that there was a very firm reaction in my own congregation and church. In fact, the vicar at the time refused to provide me with a letter of recommendation to go to the Tribunal. Members of the congregation, a lot of them, were definitely changed in their attitude towards me. As an ordinand I had previously read the lesson every Sunday but now this suddenly stopped.

One settled in Trealaw, Barrie and Sheila Naylor quickly became immersed in their social work task.

BARRIE NAYLOR

> Unemployment had been a real problem, especially in the Rhondda and south Wales. That's why the Quakers were there, to help relieve unemployment. The Settlement supplied all sorts of services such as crafts, dressmaking, Boys' and Girls' Clubs. It wasn't called social work at the time but the Settlement at Maes yr Haf became a centre for all sorts of activity. It was quite an outstanding example of service to others. William and Emma Noble were the wardens there.

SHEILA NAYLOR

> In 1927, after the General Strike, Emma Noble went down to see the plight of the miners. She'd heard somebody at the yearly Quaker meeting in Manchester describe how awful it was. She had what we call 'a concern' and so she went down and devoted the rest of her life to it. And her husband.

MAES-YR-HAF  EDUCATIONAL  SETTLEMENT
TREALAW, RHONDDA, GLAMORGAN, S. WALES

Maes yr Haf yearbook

She got relief services going and let the rest of the Quakers know there was a diet problem there. They had clothing and all sorts of things sent down from Quaker meetings all over the country. The Unemployed Men's Clubs were the big thing that the Nobles invented, all over the valleys. They were supplied by the Settlement with all sorts of things, like leather for mending shoes, wood to make furniture. And they gave lectures on all types of things. It gave them something to live for.

For John Cledan Mears the result of his first Tribunal appearance was far from satisfactory. The decision was, 'No evidence of conscience.'

JOHN CLEDAN MEARS

Well, that made me sub-human, didn't it? Intimidation lands you in that predicament, but it wasn't enough to change my conviction. I stood by that conviction and I was able, privileged in fact, to attend an Appellate Tribunal in Cardiff. My case was simply that those who go to war and myself, who refuses to go to war, have the same end – namely peace. It's just that the means to that end are different.

The grounds that I was made exempt at the Appellate Tribunal was that I was engaged in theological studies. I went on to take my degree at Oxford and then do research – so in that way I was complying with what they wanted. I wasn't asked to do war work, work that would have helped the war effort. But I would have done it.

The work of the Settlement at Trealaw continued throughout the war and well beyond. It was fascinating and compelling work and people like the Nobles and the Naylors found that it was difficult to leave.

SHEILA NAYLOR

We did meals for evacuees during the war. There was a school evacuated to a large house next door and so the women members of the Settlement were organised by Emma Noble into producing meals every day for these evacuees. They all came in, a hundred or so at a time, and they were given a wonderful two-course meal for just sixpence.

The Settlement itself was a large Victorian house with about two acres of land right up against the mountainside. It was a lovely spot.

BARRIE NAYLOR

It was officially known as the Maes yr Haf Education Settlement. But in the Rhondda, locally, they always referred to the place as 'The Quakers'. Thirty years we stayed there, thirty years in all, until we retired in 1971.

SHEILA NAYLOR

When we left in 1971, when we retired, we thought there wasn't going to be any more unemployment. We left the Rhondda as an affluent society. It didn't last.

JOHN CLEDAN MEARS

If you take a stand you have to defend what you stand for. I don't think I was being brave but I felt I had to make this stand. It did seem gigantic – if that's the word – at the time. It was literally a question of life and death – the life and death of individuals, the life and death of civilisations, the life and death of the religious conviction that has governed my whole life.

My father, in his quiet way, gave me all the support possible. And my mother, when she witnessed the reaction of the church, said, 'If that's the church I wouldn't bother.'

For me, the conviction that I held then holds now. And do you know, the very fact that I had a choice whether to fight or not, was a tribute to the country and the civilisation in which I found myself and in which I was brought up.

Many people in Wales found themselves in reserved occupations during the war, working in jobs that were essential to the war effort. Sometimes it was possible to replace a large part of the workforce with women, with conscientious objectors or even prisoners-of-war. The use of Land Army girls was just one example of this.

However, for some skilled workers there was no chance of replacement. Their war, their way of fighting the totalitarian regimes of Germany and Italy, would be to continue with their normal peace-time jobs, content in the knowledge that they were making an invaluable contribution to the war effort.

The mining and munitions industries were two areas that demanded a highly-skilled workforce. HARRY RADCLIFFE and HARRY HIGHMAN were just two people who worked in these industries during the war. And both of them understood the vital nature of their jobs.

Men in reserved occupations during the war worked in factories, mines and, sometimes, shipyards.

HARRY RADCLIFFE

I'd been a miner since the age of fourteen. During the war we worked seven days a week, sometimes, in the Wyndham Colliery. The coal was used for the Royal Navy – it didn't make black smoke, so they could get away with coming closer to the enemy than if they used other types of coal. South Wales coal was the best mining coal in the world. It was as vital to produce that coal as it was to produce ammunition and everything else.

The miners of this country gave everything, all the miners of south Wales. Production of coal was as vital as any fighting unit.

HARRY HIGHMAN

I went to Newport Tech. for a year when I left school, until I was sixteen. I decided I wanted to be a fitter and turner. Our neighbour worked at Caerwent and he said, 'Why don't you go there? They've got an excellent programme. They're really interested in training lads, not looking for cheap labour. You'll get a full training programme there.'

I started there in September 1943. They were manufacturing cordite for propellant, used for naval guns and ammunition. The requirement was something like 150 tons a week so it was quite an intensive labour operation.

It was quite hazardous as well. We were making nitric acid, sulphuric acid, nitroglycerine, so fire was always a danger. We had special shoes to wear and protective clothing – and women weren't allowed silk underwear because static electricity could cause an accident.

HARRY RADCLIFFE

I wouldn't say safety was compromised but, perhaps, the man at the coalface wouldn't have quite the right amount of material. One day, a mines inspector came round and we were short of material like pit props. We'd have to stretch a bit further than the law really allowed. That's when the mines inspector said, 'We're losing men in the forces, we can afford to lose one or two underground.' That's the only compromise we ever made. Everything else had to go by the terms of the Mines Act.

HARRY HIGHMAN

One of the reasons for choosing Caerwent as a munitions factory was that it lay in a bit of a valley. If you drive from Newport, particularly in the morning, the whole area is often covered in mist. Whether that was the reason for choosing it, I don't know, but the factory was never bombed. There were something like 700 buildings there, all in a 2000-acre site, but it was never bombed.

The main reason they chose Caerwent was the water. They needed three million gallons of water a day. It came from the Severn Tunnel – I believe they pump nine million gallons out of that tunnel each day. During the war, they piped it to Caerwent, into huge reservoirs.

The work of miners and munitions workers was gratefully recognised by the government. Manny Shinwell, the Minister for Fuel, was clear that the miners played as important a role in the war as the fighting men at the front. And sometimes their contribution gained formal approval from people like Royalty.

HARRY RADCLIFFE

I was working afternoons and went to the baths to get changed before going down the pit. The colliery manager had left instructions that everyone had to be out of the baths by 1.30 as, at 2.00, we were having special visitors. The King and Queen were coming to open the pithead baths. They'd been in use for some time but this was the official opening.

After the ceremony the King and Queen visited the new winding-house, about a quarter of a mile on towards the pit. I stood with my lamp, along with two other men, Jack Adams and Ralph Arlett. On their way back from the winding-house, the Queen came over to me and asked if I was married. I said I was. And she asked, 'How has your family managed with the rations?' I just said, 'I'm sorry but that's nothing to do with me. That's my wife's department.' I didn't know what else to say. But she smiled as she walked away. I was really taken aback – you don't expect them to come and talk to you like that.

Harry Radcliffe meets the Queen (later the Queen Mother).

I went to work next morning and all the boys were saying 'On the Pathe News at the cinema last night, we saw you talking to the Queen.' Normal Lewis, our Welsh champion boxer, he saw it up in Blackpool. And then, on the Saturday night, I went to the cinema and they put it on, special, because I was there. Everyone stood up and clapped me.

HARRY HIGHMAN

There was a great atmosphere at Caerwent. People in those days lived for each other. If someone was in trouble, had bad news, say, you'd talk, console them. A lot of things were in short supply. You'd go into work and maybe you hadn't shaved. Somebody would say, 'Why haven't you shaved?' 'Well, I haven't got a blade.' The next day two or three people would bring you in razor blades. Or food – 'I'll bring you a couple of eggs.' There was a great family spirit. People lived, helped and worked for each other.

The munitions factories might have been civilian establishments but they were run on strict military lines. Safety was paramount. As Harry Highman says, 'If it wasn't safe you didn't do it.' Even pay day was run in a clearly autocratic manner.

HARRY HIGHMAN

When we were paid, it was ten minutes before clocking-out time. You would have to line up in the sequence of your works numbers. If you were, say, 701 you'd be first, 702 would be second and so on. You'd have a long line, perhaps a hundred people, and if you weren't in your correct number sequence, they wouldn't pay you. You'd have to go to the end of the line and wait until everyone else had been paid. It was a strict, sort of Sergeant-Major-style pay parade.

HARRY RADCLIFFE

In the mines you were getting two and sixpence for each ton of coal – nothing for the small coal that went with it, only the large coal. Whatever you cut, you'd get paid for. And I had to pay my boy – the Bevin Boy who was helping me – out of that. Sometimes we'd have a bad week and then we'd only pick up two or three pounds.

HARRY HIGHMAN

At lunchtime we played Solo. We had half an hour lunch break so you'd rush in, eat your food and then a gang of apprentices would play Solo – halfpenny, penny, tuppence, according to the hand. We didn't put any money out, just kept a tally. And at the end of the week, if you'd won sixpence you'd have done really well.

The Welsh people had always maintained excellent relationships with the Italians who lived amongst them. The Italian cafes or coffee shops were so popular in the valleys that the image has now become almost a cliché. For many years Italian men, women and children had also been selling ice cream around the doors of Welsh communities. Their cafes provided a haven for out-of-work miners and steel workers during the Depression and were as much a part of Welsh life as Miners' Institutes, chapels and rugby clubs.

However, Mussolini declared war on Britain in 1940 and almost immediately the Welsh-Italians became suspect. Fear of fifth columnists and spies – a fear that was considerably greater than the reality – meant that within days of Mussolini's declaration, over 4000 Italians were behind bars. The Brachis and Sidolis, people who had lived as part of the Welsh towns and villages for more years than anyone cared to remember, were suddenly rounded up and taken away to transit camps and, eventually, to the Isle of Man. The original plan was that, from there, all Italian and German aliens would be sent to Canada where, it was felt, they would cause little trouble.

MARCO CARINI, from Beaufort in Ebbw Vale, remembers with terrible clarity the moment when his father was taken away.

MARCO CARINI

> They came and fetched him at gunpoint in the night. The policeman hammered on the door as if we were criminals. My father thought something had happened – he hadn't a clue that he was going to be arrested. We all got out of bed, wondering what was happening. I was a little boy of six and that was the last time I saw my father for eleven months.
>
> The local sergeant, Sergeant Morgan, he was nice when he got inside. He told my mother and father, 'Sorry I got to do it, Jake.' He called him Jake – it was really Giaccomo, Jake for short. 'I've got to do it. It's my duty.'
>
> We came down the stairs to see what was happening. Mam said, 'Get back up the stairs.' Dad said, 'No, no, leave them here. It's the last time I'll see them until we don't know when.' So we had a cwtch and a cuddle and then he was taken out through the door by Sergeant Morgan.

For PETER SIDOLI the experience was a little different. He had been in Wales since 1936, living in Caerau near Maesteg, and helping out his parents with their ice cream business.

PETER SIDOLI

> When war broke out the local sergeant came to see my father and said, 'Look Sid, I'm very sorry but you know the war's broken out. I've got the authority to intern your two sons, Luigi and Francesco, because they're of military age. But you, Sid, I won't intern you. But you'll have to move from Caerau because you're only a few miles from the sea and from Bridgend and the armament factory.'
>
> We didn't know where to go but Sergeant Bloom said 'Haven't you got any relatives?' My father phoned my uncle in Abercynon and he said, 'I'm the only

one here, with two shops. All my partners have been interned. There's plenty of room; we're glad for you to come.' That's where we went. Within a month or two my uncle got interned as well, so my father then controlled the two shops until the end of the war.

In the towns of Wales there was very little resentment towards the Italians. Germany and the Nazi regime were universally detested but towards the friendly, happy Italians there was, in the main, only understanding and acceptance.

Sidoli's shop in Caerau

PETER SIDOLI

After we had been in Abercynon a few months, my father had a letter from the Home Office. It said that if he wanted, he could go back to Caerau and open his café again, because it would help the war effort. That's the truth, from the Home Office! But we didn't go. We stuck in Abercynon. My father said, 'Until the war's finished we stay here.' And that's what happened.

MARCO CARINI

Most of the community were very good. There were a couple of families, further afield, who lost people in the war and they

The Carini brothers: from left to right Luigi (Lou), Guiseppe (Joe), Giaccomo (Jake), Francesco (Frank) – Francesco and Guiseppe perished when the *Arandora Star* was torpedoed.

blamed us. 'Go back home,' they'd say. But you took it with a pinch of salt.
You'd get a couple of hotheads coming into the shop now and then – my
mother kept the shop going – and you'd maybe get some bad language. 'Italian
Bastards!' and all that nonsense – if they were drunk. We never had any
windows broken or anything.

PETER SIDOLI

You'd get a few fellows, they'd call you names like 'Macaroni'. I never took
any notice of it. The teacher in Abercynon, Mr Richards, first day at school he
called me upstairs to his office. 'Peter,' he said, 'the war is on and children can
be very cruel, you know, whether they're Italian, Welsh or English. You may
have problems because of the war. They may bully you a bit. Don't react, but if
you come to a position where you can't carry it, come and see me. And I'll see
what I can do about it.'

I thought to myself, 'That's good, that's wonderful. That's a real teacher.'
But to tell you the truth I never had any bullying, nothing. I was part of the
school.

For many of the Italians who had been interned – and for German refugees who
suffered the same fate at this time – the first stop was the Isle of Man.

Mario Carini aboard his father's ice cream wagon in Beaufort, near Ebbw Vale, at the start of the war.

PETER SIDOLI

> I'll always remember the front at Douglas on the Isle of Man because it was literally taken over by the internees, the aliens. They were kept there in the different hotels. Some of the most famous Italians were there, all the top cooks and chefs, whatever. I visited my brothers twice in the Isle of Man.

MARCO CARINI

> My father said that conditions on the Isle of Man were terrible: scratching for bread, nothing on the floor, very rough. The soldiers treated them all right; they got to know them and would scrounge a sly fag off them. But when the officers came round they had to be strict.

For some of the Italian and German internees, however, the consequences of the war and internment were far more serious, far more tragic. The liner *Arandora Star* was taking the first of them to Canada when she was torpedoed by a U-boat off the coast of Ireland on 2nd July, 1940. Only 859 survived, many of them picked up by the Canadian destroyer HMCS *St Laurent*. Over 700 internees died in the oil-streaked waters.

MARCO CARINI

> My three uncles were all interned, all arrested together, at the same time. My father went to the Isle of Man but the other three were put on the *Arandora Star*. Of course she was torpedoed and went down.
>
> The story is that Uncle Luigi jumped off the ship and survived. But either Guisseppi or Franco, I don't know which, went back to get his false teeth and the other one went with him. They both went down with the ship. Their families were bitter for a long time with the British government for allowing the boat to sail.
>
> Luigi said it had been terrible on the *Arandora Star*. There was always fighting between the Italians and the Germans over who had the most food. They weren't on the ship many days before it sank.

PETER SIDOLI

> I lost a relative on the *Arandora Star*. He came from Swansea, name of Rossi. He held his brother for hours on a plank of wood. Then he couldn't hold him any longer. I think there were about 42 from Bardi who went down on her.
>
> Regarding the internment, 90% of Welsh people will tell you it shouldn't have happened because Italians were part of the community. But I understand it, I understand it well. In time of war you've got to do these things to protect what you believe in.

Release from internment came with peace, or once Italy had surrendered. Even then, many internees had to continue with war work for some time. Peter Sidoli's brothers worked on farms around the Maesteg area for a further twelve months after their

release, before returning to the family business. Marco Carini's father had been
lucky; he came home a lot earlier.

MARCO CARINI

> When my father came back, the war was still on. He had more support from
> people than anything else. When the soldiers came home on leave they'd be
> straight in, talking to my father. He'd help keep them in cigarettes. The Italian
> community was all against Mussolini for going in with the Germans. He
> caused a lot of suffering, a great loss of life. A lot of families are still upset
> about it, even now.

German aliens – most of them refugees from Hitler's regime – had been interned
along with the Italians. As the war drew to a close, Wales began to see many more
Germans – prisoners of war who had been captured following the D-Day landings.
Many of these young men were sent to work on Welsh farms, adding to the
workforce, producing food for the nation. WYN TREPTE and MAX
TSCHACKERT were two POWs who were sent to Wales as the war ended and who
stayed on afterwards.

WYN TREPTE

> I was in the Hitler Youth and, as a lot of
> the leaders were called up to the army,
> the leadership of the Hitler Youth became
> younger and younger. Before I was called
> up I was in charge of a company.
>
> I went to a Hitler Youth Leaders'
> Camp and the *kommandant*, an SS
> officer, persuaded me to volunteer as an
> officer cadet. I only had six weeks
> training and went to the front, the
> Russian front. But I wasn't there long,
> only about six months before our
> regiment was rubbed out. I was one of
> just six to come out.
>
> Because I was an officer cadet they
> pushed me to a new unit, called the Hitler
> Youth Division. They needed NCOs so
> we were doing NCO duty with new
> recruits. I wasn't much older than them.
> The Hitler Youth Division went into
> Normandy when the invasion started. I
> got there on 7th July and on 19th July I
> was captured by the Royal Welsh
> Fusiliers.

Wyn Trepte pictured soon after his
arrival in the Machynlleth area after
the war.

## MAX TSCHACKERT

I joined the air force in 1937. I wanted to go as flying personnel but I had bad teeth. I'd trained as a baker and, as a baker, you breathed in the sugar. Bad for the teeth. So I wasn't fit for it. I was in the Medical Corps and ended up as a Regimental Sergeant Major. Then, in 1944, they transferred me to the army. They didn't have enough personnel in the army. And the air force? It was bankrupt – no aeroplanes any more.

I was captured on 14th February, 1945 – 'Come out, you bloody Nazi baby!' That's what they called. Actually I was in a house and the woman upstairs was shouting, 'Get out from here, they'll shoot us as well.' So, of course, we did. Hands up, that was it.

I had a ring, a signet ring. It was ripped off my finger. The finger could have gone as well. And my wristwatch. Gone.

Max Tschackert in the uniform of a Regimental Sergeant Major in the Luftwaffe.

## WYN TREPTE

After being in the holding camps they put us on a ferry that ran from Ostende to Dover. They took us to Kempton Park racecourse where everything was turned over to the reception of prisoners of war – de-lousing, registering, fingerprints, photographs.

We moved around a lot – Edinburgh, Rugely, Salisbury Plain. Then Chepstow. From Chepstow they took us up to Newtown where I was cooking in the officer's mess. Then they moved me to Pennal. Once they found out I'd been cooking in the mess they asked me to cook for them there.

## MAX TSCHACKERT

I was in prison camps in Belgium. So many of them. They changed us around from one camp to another. If you were in Camp 22 this week, next week it was Camp 25. So you didn't know where you were. It was too easy to disappear, see.

Then they brought us to London and put us on the station. All you could hear was 'Five, ten, fifteen, twenty.' If you weren't quick enough they'd kick you up the arse. I'm not saying we didn't do it – most probably our fellows did too.

They sent us to Newport, guarded all the way. They must have thought we'd kill any bugger we met! When we got to Brecon we were searched. Everything out of your pockets, in front of everyone, there on the platform. And then we went in a lorry to Bwlch.

Wyn Trepte and Max Tschackert spent the next few years working as labourers on farms in the Machynlleth and Brecon areas. When the war ended, they had the opportunity to return to Germany but neither of them took the chance.

WYN TREPTE

> Once you were repatriated they took you back to Germany. For those who stayed, you went into civilian status but you had to sign a contract to work on the farms for ten years. Well, I'd had letters and parcels from my mother before the end of the war but then there was a big raid on the town and, after that, I had nothing at all.
>
> One day, it was two and a half years after I signed the contract, I was cutting thistles on the top of the mountain and suddenly I knew that I had a letter. I came down for lunch and there it was, from my mother. How I knew I'm not quite sure. But the letter was from my mother, saying she was still alive. And from then on we corresponded again.

MAX TSCHACKERT

> I made the best of it. I had no home any more. Breslau was gone. My private things left in the barracks in Germany had been bombed out. I had nothing, nothing.
>
> In 1946 I wrote, in May, to Breslau, to my parents. I never heard back. Then I received a card – on 15th December, 1957. It was from the Red Cross – my mother's writing. Eleven years later! It must have been in the system all that time.

Working on the farms was not an easy task for the German prisoners of war. For some of them it was far too much – as EILUNED REES of Llansteffan recalls.

EILUNED REES

> It was a Sunday morning, a very cold, bitter morning. The ground was covered in snow and I was dressing in front of the fire when the phone went. It was a phone call saying that a prisoner of war had escaped from one of the farms and that my father would have to go out and look for him. My father, of course, was the local policeman.

Eiluned's father set off on his motorbike, searching for the POW. Her mother decided to keep her at home, instead of going to chapel as usual.

EILUNED REES

> So I was sitting there, curled up in front of the fire, my mother preparing breakfast, when a knock came at the door. And there was a poor young man, absolutely soaking and very distressed. He was the prisoner of war who'd run away. Other people had taken over the farm and although he'd been well treated by the original people, he wasn't so well treated by the new ones. He was cold, wet and miserable and hadn't been fed enough. So he'd run away and come to the only place he thought he could get refuge – the police station.

The POW was taken in. Eiluned's mother took off his shoes and socks, put his feet in a bowl of hot water and sat him front of the fire.

EILUNED REES

> My mother cooked him my father's ration of bacon and egg. The poor young man was starving. In due course my father reappeared and looked with amazement to find his quarry sitting in his chair by the fire, eating his breakfast. And about to don his socks. But he took it well. He waited until the young man was well fed and dry before he took him over to the camp.
>
> There was a very touching farewell scene, my mother crying as the young man, also in tears, thanked her. Even at that age, I wondered, 'What's all this about? Why a war between people who are exactly the same?'

Not everyone had the same enlightened views, however.

WYN TREPTE

> Sometimes there was bad feeling. I became a rep after I left the farms and this involved going to meet garage owners. Some of them had been in the war themselves. And sometimes they would turn aside from you. You couldn't blame them, because some of them had lost family in the war. Who else was there to blame?

MAX TSCHACKERT

> Of course they called us names – 'Bloody bugger', *schweinhund* – swear words, things like that. But then, some of the people were nice. One of the farmers I worked for – remember, we had no pay, just £4.10s a week from the War Department – one of the farmers, we'd finish on Saturday at twelve o'clock, and he'd give me twenty Senior Service and a couple of apples. That put me right over the weekend.
>
> I married a Welsh woman, from here in the village, the postman's daughter. So I went to the sawmill in Bwlch. He said, 'Your rate is £4.2s.8d – according to your ability you shall have more.' I became the church warden, I was secretary in the gardening association. I joined everything. Some people, they called me a 'Bloody German' – in the beginning. But when you tell them, when you challenge them, they go yellow.

Despite minor problems, living in Wales was a lot better than life in Germany after the war.

WYN TREPTE

> In 1955 my mother came out of the Russian Zone to see a nephew of hers. In those days you could come out into the west, no trouble. She asked me to go out and see her so I made the arrangements and I went, from Machynlleth, to see her for a week.

They had practically nothing to eat after the war. They'd had a hell of a time. Later, the Russians put restrictions on people going in and coming out. You couldn't blame them for that. Their wealth was labour and they couldn't afford to lose labour. A lot of workers were scarpering to the west. They couldn't afford it.

Anyway, my mother joined me in 1970 and she lived with me for ten years. She died in Machynlleth.

Learning English was important and both Wyn Trepte and Max Tscheckert did it in different ways.

MAX TSCHECKERT

When my daughter was in Grammar School, she took German. Every time she came home with homework, German homework, it was 'Dad, what's this? What do they mean by that?' I explained it. And little did she know – that's how I learned my English as well. I wasn't well educated, you understand. Germany was in a terrible condition after the First World War. It was all different in those days. We had to earn a living, make money. Remember, I'd gone to school in 1923. I had no education, nothing at all. Too many in the class, 40 or 50. The teacher, he never even knew all the names of all the class, poor bugger.

WYN TREPTE

I was determined to learn English. I had a good book in the POW camp which gave lessons but it wasn't enough for me, I wanted to do it quicker. At night I used to write down twenty words and take them to work the following day. On the farm – well, you didn't have to use your head much, just your brawn. By the time night came I could speak them, read them and spell them. In a week I had 140 new words.

Wyn Trepte and Max Tscheckert were just two of the German POWs who made their home in Wales after the war. They were part of a new, vibrant and dynamic society – a society that had been changed, for ever, by the events of 1939-45.

## THE WELSH ADOPTION

It was not by choice that I came to Wales
As a youth from a different race,
Nor was I inclined to stay and face
Much time in this forsaken place.

As a prisoner of war and twenty-one,
deprived of privilege and mind undone,
Why should I care for bards and rhyme,
Loving, dancing, singing and time?

Yes, time became the instrument to lance that festering sore
Of hate. Yes hate and disillusionment were cut right to the core.

In time I learned to love this land
Where rivers run, where mountains stand
Like choir boys in rows and rows
That sing of Wales in Sunday clothes.

Now I love the singing of this nation,
The bards, the poets and their quotations.
Now in fact I'm Welsh
By choice and inclination.

(poem written by Wyn Trepte, German POW)

*Chapter Nine*

# From Sea to Mines

During the Second World War thousands of men and women were called up to fight in the armed forces, including the Royal Navy. Still more served in the Merchant Marine, braving Hitler's U-boats to bring vital food, supplies and weapons to Britain.

In many respects, the sailors of the Merchant Navy were facing the most extreme dangers of all. Their ships were, in the main, unarmed and sauntered along at under ten knots. They might be sailing in convoys but they were still sitting targets for enemy submarines. So deadly was the U-boat menace that, on two occasions, Germany almost succeeded in cutting off the vital supply of food coming into Britain. By the spring of 1941, the country was just weeks away from starvation.

The following year, 1942, was almost as bad. U-boats were sinking merchant ships faster than Britain and America could build replacements. Through it all, the sailors of Britain's Merchant Navy continued their dangerous and vitally important task. It was a task that sailors like JIM ARNOLD and RAY NEWBERRY took in their stride.

JIM ARNOLD

I suppose I was one of the fortunate few. In the course of the war I was on nine different ships. And except for one, all of them were sunk after I'd left them.

We all had our little bags where you put a bit of this and a bit of that so, if you were torpedoed and you had to abandon ship, you'd grab that. You had your certificates in there and usually a bottle of amber-coloured liquid – in case you needed it in the lifeboats.

But you know, even when there was torpedoing going on and depth charging, I still climbed into my pyjamas and went to sleep at night. I put it all out of my mind. In my mind's eye I could see the green hills of Pembrokeshire and I'd think of those and drift quietly off to sleep.

"Don't trouble to dress any further, Mum perhaps I didn't see a U-Boat after all!"

Sailors liked to hold on to their reputation as ladies' men, despite all dangers.

RAY NEWBERRY

> I don't think you ever thought about torpedoes and things. The way I looked at it was, I was going to sea as a professional seafarer and I was keen to learn my business. The fact that somebody might be throwing bullets, bombs, torpedoes or whatever, was purely incidental to the business of learning my trade.
>
> And, of course, when you're seventeen, things don't look half so dangerous as they do when you're seventy-seven. You don't really recognise danger too much. You thought, well, if we should be unlucky then the lifeboats are there – we'll sail into port in one of those.

Jim Arnold had left St David's in Pembrokeshire to go to sea before the war began. In his words, he didn't want to be a country hick forever in St David's. When war broke out he was in the Pacific Ocean.

JIM ARNOLD

> We were steaming along the American coast of the Pacific, to a little port called Astoria in Oregon, to land timber for Japan. When war broke out the first thing the Chinese crew did was to paint everything dull grey – funnel, masts, everything. Little did we realise at the time that that would be the colour for the next six, dangerous years.

RAY NEWBERRY

> I went to sea in 1944 as a cadet – that's the lowest form of human life on board ship! My first ship was the ex *Dusseldorf* of Bremen – a German ship. She'd been picked up in the South Atlantic and brought back to this country. She was re-named *Poland* for a little while, then after a month or so she was renamed again, *Empire Confidence*.
>
> I joined her at Middlesbrough and we sailed in a convoy, down the east coast, up into the Solent. We anchored there and picked up another convoy. Then we went through the Dover Straits to Milford Haven.
>
> In that area attacks came, generally, from German E Boats – fast motor gunboats. They could run rings around merchant ships, of course. E Boats or aerial attack.

The convoy system had been used during the First World War when it proved to be highly successful against the U-boats. When war broke out again in 1939, the system was re-introduced.

JIM ARNOLD

> It was only after the collapse of France in 1940 that things really hotted up, as far as we were concerned. It was quite usual to have forty or so ships in a convoy. If there were forty ships, there'd be ten columns of four ships each – not four columns of ten ships. It was a broad front.
>
> The first thing you had to do, on joining a convoy, was find your number. If you were 3:1 that meant you'd be the lead ship in the third column, 3:2 would

be behind you. The Commodore's ship would either be in the middle column or, if there were even columns, in the one to the right of the middle column. Keep an eye on him.

Jim Arnold is clear that the old adage of the speed of the convoy being the speed of the slowest ship isn't strictly true.

JIM ARNOLD

If it was, say, a ten-knot convoy – and that was actually a very fast convoy for merchant ships – then they all had to maintain ten knots. If they didn't, they'd fall back. If they broke down it was just too bad. Because you couldn't slow down a forty-ship convoy to just one knot – that would be suicidal.

In the convoy instructions would be the North Atlantic Chart. It would have three positions on it. A, B or C. And after the noon position each day, the Commodore would signal, 'Rendezvous for the day after tomorrow will be X degrees, X miles, from A, B or C.' So any ship that had to stop for engine repairs, when she finally got underway she could try and head to this position and rejoin the convoy.

RAY NEWBERRY

We went round to Milford, which was a forming-up place for convoys. We were going to the East. I think most of the North Atlantic convoys seemed to go up to Liverpool area and then sail north of Ireland. As we weren't crossing the western ocean, as we were going down south, heading for Gibraltar, we formed up at Milford Haven. Then, when we were ready, we sailed and away we went for the East, via the Mediterranean.

The Royal Navy provided escorts for the convoys, usually in the shape of destroyers, corvettes or anti-aircraft cruisers.

RAY NEWBERRY

Oh, the escorts were always knocking about. You didn't tend to see a great deal of them because they didn't hang around in the middle of a convoy. They were usually on the periphery of the whole organisation, working on the basis that things don't necessarily happen in the middle. They would detect it before it reached the middle of the convoy – a submarine or whatever.

The U-boat threat was quite significant. But, of course, it wasn't exactly plain sailing all the time either. The Atlantic weather takes no account of whether you're German, Italian, Japanese, American, British, whatever.

One time it was so bad that the convoy broke up and we steamed on to Gibraltar on our own. Once the convoy split up, you went at maximum speed and we had quite a bit in hand. I suppose the average speed of a merchant ship was about eight or nine knots. In the *Dusseldorf* we could turn in thirteen or fourteen knots. So, of course, we were able to make our own way into Gibraltar. We got there before the rest of them showed up.

JIM ARNOLD

> We had naval escorts, of course. Usually they'd be well ahead of the convoy, searching for submarines. Occasionally they would come up close to us but usually they left the convoy role to the Commodore.
>
> Some of the ships that protected us, initially at least, were no more than glorified trawlers. We didn't have great faith in them but things improved as the years went by.

Danger, when it came, seemed something that had to be endured. And often it was the little things, the tiny pieces of detail or the amusing incident, that the sailors remember.

JIM ARNOLD

> We were bombed by Condors, off Finistere, once. We were the Commodore's ship at the time – we wished to God he'd move off elsewhere – and we had the ack-ack cruiser alongside us.
>
> What surprised me at the time were the near misses. They'd give the vessel a ten to fifteen degree list before she'd flop back down onto an even keel. So we were rather pleased that they were near misses and nothing else.

RAY NEWBERRY

> We had to have a patch put on our mainmast. It was caused by an excited gunner following an aircraft. As the plane flew past, the mast passed between the gunner and the plane. When you're concentrating on trying to bring down the enemy you don't think about things that might get in the way. And this time the mast got in the way. Really, he severed the top of the mainmast and so we had the patch put on, a collar about two foot deep, right the way around.
>
> At the same time we had that done, we also had rails fitted around the Orlikon pits. We had four Orilkon guns on the ship and these rails prevented the Orlikon from firing to hit the funnel, the masts, the chaps standing down on the poop deck aft and the chap standing on the bridge.
>
> It was so easy to fire bullets close to those people if you were concentrating on aircraft. After all, we weren't gunners, who knew what they were doing. We were just trying to get the blooming aeroplane.

Merchant ships like Ray Newberry's *Empire Confidence* were sometimes equipped with small calibre weapons, although how people thought they were going to fight off submarines or surface raiders with just one old gun was never fully explained.

JIM ARNOLD

> When we arrived in Hong Kong they put a four point seven on the poop. We all had to get knuckled down into gunnery training. In those days there were no DEMS gunners, like there were later, on board. They were conscripts in charge of gunnery but up until that time we all had to do it. My job was sight setter. I had to yell, 'Sights moving, sights set.'
>
> We only got ammunition for the gun at Gibraltar. Up until then we had the gun but nothing to fire.

Submarines were an ever-present concern for the officers on the merchant ships. Nobody knew when they would appear and, normally, nobody ever saw them – or heard them – until it was too late.

RAY NEWBERRY

On that convoy from Milford Haven three ships didn't arrive at Gibraltar. Which ones they were we didn't know. We didn't hear anything happen to them. I don't recall hearing any explosions. There were all sorts of things going off and you never worried too much about it. In fact, it used to be the chaps in the engine room who would ring up to the bridge and say, 'Is that a bomb?' You hadn't heard anything. They'd get the shockwaves underwater. It impressed upon the hull of the ship and, of course, they'd heard it in the engine room. Up on top, in the fresh air, we didn't hear anything. That happened several times.

Often the danger came in a different form – perhaps surface raiders like the *Scharnhorst*, *Gneisenau* and *Graf Spee*; perhaps in the shape of gales and wild weather; or sometimes, in the form of mines and minefields.

JIM ARNOLD

I once sailed with old Tommy Bell and he told me a story about his ship, the *Chilean Reefer*. She couldn't keep up with the convoy because of heavy weather; she didn't have the power. She was twenty miles or so behind the convoy when a warship appeared and signalled her to stop. The recognition signal was missing so Tommy Bell knew it was an enemy ship. It was the *Gneisenau*, in fact. *The Chilean Reefer* turned and fled, sending out the RRR signal – Raider, Raider, Raider.

The *Gneisenau* was firing and Tommy Bell had the audacity to fire back with a little 4.7. Eighty-seven salvos the Gneisenau fired before they blew the *Chilean Reefer* out of the water. Two boats got away, the Second Mate in charge of one of them, Tommy Bell in charge of the other. The Second Mate went on board the *Gneisenau* as they wanted to interrogate him to find out what kind of ship this was.

All of a sudden she went astern, at speed, and somebody shouted from the *Gneisenau*, 'We'll be back.' Two hours later Tommy Bell, in mid winter off Iceland, with wounded people in the boat, thought she really had returned. But it was a Royal Naval vessel and so Tommy and his crew were brought on board.

The action of the tiny ship that had the effrontery to stand up to a battle cruiser could have made a great story but it was kept quiet.

Mines were a perpetual problem. And, unlike the U-boats and surface raiders, they did not go away once peace came in 1945. GEORGE BLAKE sailed out of Trafford Warf in Manchester at the end of the war and arrived at Queen Alexandra Dock in Cardiff a few days later. They were heading for Malta.

GEORGE BLAKE

Mines were the biggest problem we faced. Our ship had what they called degousing gear which was for use against magnetic mines. We used to put on the degousing gear and it was intended to neutralise the ship's magnetism so that she wouldn't activate these magnetic mines.

RAY NEWBERRY

All merchant ships had a device for dealing with mines. When I say 'device', what we had was an A frame over the bow which you could lower into the water. It had a sort of bucket on it which set up a hammering to set off acoustic mines.

Then we had paravanes which we could stream over the bow and they would keep us safe from moored mines because the

The *Empire Confidence* (formerly the Dusseldorf): note the A frame over her bows.

paravane would sweep the mine away. We also had a degousing system which, broadly speaking, was a powerful electric coil running around the ship, on the ship's side. It created a current which counteracted the magnetic mine. The trouble was it also counteracted your magnetic compass.

GEORGE BLAKE

When we were going through a minefield we went to the naval people in Liverpool and they used to give us a route. We'd plot it on the chart. The trouble was, in heavy weather, some of the buoys of the channel would drift and it was a bit difficult to pick them up in their current position. The only ship I ever knew that was sunk by mines after the war was in Algeceras Bay, off Gibraltar. There were probably others but that's the only one I know about.

The weather in the Atlantic Ocean was always treacherous, no matter what the season or time of year.

JIM ARNOLD

We were steaming for Australia but we had to join a convoy. Our intention was to break off at a suitable point and head down to South Africa. Eventually we ran into a tremendous north-westerly gale.

It was such a horrible sea that the order came, 'Convoy scatter and proceed independently.' By that time it was so dangerous that we couldn't heave to and turn around so we just ran with the wind and sea behind us.

We'd slide down into those valleys and sides of green water. And we'd think, 'How are we going to get out of this? Don't look aft, there's somebody following us.' We'd see this huge wave behind us and we'd say, 'Come on girl, get your bum up.' She did and then she'd slide down under again. It was frightening. I can still recall it clearly.

Mostly, the daily routine went on, unhindered. Men worked on the engines or on deck, officers kept watch and tried to avoid the U-boats.

RAY NEWBERRY

As the two cadets on board, we were both watch-keeping. I hasten to say that I was just the boy standing in the corner. I wasn't qualified to do anything. One of us used to keep the 12.00 till 4.00 watch and the other would take the 4.00 to 8.00 watch. That gave an additional pair of eyes during those two watches.

When we were in the North Atlantic and the threat was rather more imminent we used to do a watch and watch about – in other words we'd do four hours on and four hours off. There was always a lot of signalling to do on the bridge, in a convoy. So, of course, we were the signallers, amongst other things.

Leisure was important to men who spent their lives under constant pressure. Sometimes a run ashore, when the ship finally reached its destination, was enough to revitalise tired limbs and ease stretched nerves. Sometimes, just meeting with different cultures brought a smile to a sailor's lips, as happened to Jim Arnold in America.

The *Empire Confidence* football team. Ray Newberry is on the right of the front row.

JIM ARNOLD

A car pulled up. I had no idea that the town was three or four miles away. Anyway, a car stopped and an elderly couple said, 'Are you boys from the British ship? Would you like a ride into town?'

Instead, they took us home and he said, 'Mother, switch the lights out. Can you see this luminous alarm clock?' He must have thought we lived in the wilds of Siberia or somewhere.

On the way back to the ship, the old man said, 'Now this is the bad part of town. It's where all the loose women live. They follow the salmon fishermen down the coast. We have our own name for them here but, of course, in England you call them Protestants!' We didn't correct him.

For Ray Newberry it was football that provided him – and his colleagues – with physical and emotional relief.

RAY NEWBERRY

When we reached India we were in Madras for quite a while. We played football against various ships out there. We got to be so good we were soon taking on shore establishments too – and we didn't lose many matches.

We were quite a good side. Amongst the crew there was one fellow – he was an assistant steward – and he'd had a trial for Grimsby Town. A junior engineer had had a trial for Sunderland and there was another engineer who'd had a trial for a team somewhere in Scotland. So we had three incredibly good players and us 'also rans'.

No matter what the pressures and strain, it did not prevent youngsters from signing on for careers at sea. There seemed to be a never-ending flow of recruits, boys who were attracted by the lure of the sea and foreign parts. CYRIL ACTIE was just one of them.

CYRIL ACTIE

After I left school I went off to sea. I was only fourteen years old and I was at sea for about two, two and a half years. Then, when I was sixteen and a half, I went fishing. I put my age up and went as a fireman on the trawlers. You had to be eighteen to be a stoker and I was only sixteen and a half. I went down and they said they wanted a trimmer and that was that. I told them I was eighteen and they accepted it. I did thirteen years, deep-sea trawling.

RAY NEWBERRY

Normally you had to do four years at sea before you were allowed to sit for your Second Mate's Certificate. In my case that was reduced because it was wartime and there was a shortage of young officers, a number having been lost. They reduced the period to three years, temporarily. And because I'd been on the *Worcester*, a recognised training ship, they gave me a year's remission. As a result I only had to do two years before I took my ticket.

As soon as you got that thin glittering gold band on your sleeve, everything changed. The first thing you did was go out and buy yourself a lot of clothes – to save having to do your own washing, to last you from port to port.

JIM ARNOLD

There's plenty of evidence that the number of fatalities during the war was heavier in the Merchant Navy than in any of the fighting forces. Oddly enough, after a ship was sunk, the deaths in lifeboats occurred at an alarming rate. It's as if the will to live, after the shock of torpedoing, had all gone. Far too many people died a lot quicker than they should have done.

Without the Americans coming in as they did, after Pearl Harbour, a lot more seamen would have lost their lives, too. I've always had a kind thought and word for America because of that.

If the armed forces and merchant navy had a romantic appeal for most youngsters, the mining industry certainly did not. And yet that was exactly where a large number of conscripts found themselves during the closing years of the war.

As early as May 1940 it was estimated that there were approximately 750,000 people working in the mining industry. The Mines Department stated that another 40,000 would be needed if output was to be raised. Higher pay and better working conditions had already induced a number of men into other industries and, despite appeals for ex miners to return to the collieries, the situation did not improve. Indeed, things were soon so desperate that the government was seriously considering the release of ex miners from the armed forces. It was estimated that nearly 82,000 men from the mines had joined the services and, by the autumn of 1943, the coal industry was still some 50,000 workers short.

Then, on 2nd December, 1943, Ernest Bevin, the Minister of Labour and National Service, addressed the House of Commons. He announced that, henceforth, when young men were called up for active service, a certain number would be selected by ballot and conscripted into the coal industry. It was the only way that the government could even begin to address the issue of manpower shortages in the mines.

The Bevin Boys scheme, as it soon became known, was profoundly unpopular and many people who had already begun training in Army and Navy cadet forces – and in the new Air Training Corps – appealed against the process. It was to no avail. Before the end of the war, 21,800 Bevin Boys had been recruited to serve in the mines.

A number of strikes by apprentices, in March 1944, gave further evidence of the unpopularity of the scheme. And in Wales, too, there were protests, as TERRY POWELL can testify.

TERRY POWELL

My brother-in-law, Lionel Wiggin, was conscripted into the mines as a Bevin Boy. He was serving his apprenticeship at the time, working for C H Baileys, the ship repairers in Barry docks. When he was called up, all the apprentices who worked with him thought it was unfair that he had to go to the mines. He'd have much preferred to go to the army or navy, something like that.

Anyway, the apprentices decided to go on strike. There were quite a few of them working there in the workshops as fitter/turner apprentices. They called the strike but, as far as I know, it was to no avail as he still went down the mines as a Bevin Boy.

Following the initial shock of learning that they would be heading for the coal mine, rather than the battleship or fighter aerodrome, most new Bevin Boys found themselves on a four-week training course. HARVEY ALFORD came from just outside Exeter and, while he was intending to try for aircrew, it was to the mines that he eventually went.

HARVEY ALFORD

I wasn't too happy about it because I'd made up my mind that I wanted to go into aircrew. But instead of going up, I had to go down – a bit of a blow really.

My parents weren't too keen on it but, on the other hand, they weren't too keen at me going into the RAF either, because that was also quite a dodgy job. My mother, who came from Cornwall, knew a little bit about mining because of the Cornish tin mines. I think she was quite satisfied or pleased that I went into the mines rather than the air force because there were quite a few that went and didn't come back.

WARWICK TAYLOR

The time came to register for call-up. Just before you were eighteen you were sent the papers to register at your local Labour Exchange. When I got there to register, keen to go into the RAF, they said, 'Sorry, but you have been balloted to go into the coal mining industry.' It was a dreadful shock.

A ballot was drawn every fortnight. Quite simply, ten slips of paper, 0-9, were placed into a bowler hat and then a number would be drawn out. If that number coincided with the last digit of your registration number, you were in the mines! There was no question of appeal. In my case, I remember my registration number, BIBJ399. Number nine was the number drawn.

I was devastated. I just couldn't believe it. I remember my mother saying, 'He's not going.' My father said, 'Of course he's got to go. It's the war effort. He's got to do his bit.'

HARVEY ALFORD

I went to Newbridge by train, then to Crumlin and stayed in a hostel for a few weeks. When we'd done our initial training, I was sent to Ogmore Vale and was in the hostel at Bryncethin. You had the option, if you wanted you could find private lodgings. All the miners said I'd be better off if I could get in with a good family. I suppose I probably had the best lodgings in south Wales. Mrs

Boden, she was like a second mother to me. She was a lovely lady. Her husband worked at the Wyndham Colliery.

For many of the young men who became Bevin Boys, it was a culture shock of unbelievable proportions. A large number of them came from middle-class backgrounds and even had white-collar jobs – in offices or shops – before their call-up.

The first day of training was a mixture of trepidation and excitement. And sometimes the jobs were not quite what they expected.

WARWICK TAYLOR

The training course would normally last four weeks. A quarter of that time would be taken up with PT with ex-army, navy and air force PT instructors. Part of the time would be in the classroom, learning about the safety aspects of working underground in a coal mine. Part of the time would be on the surface and the majority, of course, would be spent underground.

In my case, they said, 'We've got lots of snow.' There was snow everywhere. 'What we want you new Bevin Boys to do is clear the snow off the railway tracks in and around the colliery.' We were doing that for three weeks, just shovelling snow on the surface.

HARVEY ALFORD

I was working in the drift mine at Penllyngwent. With a deep mine you go down in a shaft, in a cage. But a drift mine is just an opening in the mountain and you walk down.

We walked in for about, I suppose, one and a half miles. Then it got very, very steep and you rode on trolleys. After that you walked in for another mile until you got to where you were actually working.

Lamp check token belonging to Harvey Alford.

WARWICK TAYLOR

I remember my first time down the shaft. We called it the initiation drop. The regulation speed for lowering men was thirty feet per second. But this was the initiation drop. They just let it go – seventy feet per second. It was nearly 3000 feet down and that's a heck of a drop. The instructor, the miner with us, warned us what they would do. He said, 'Bend your knees, it won't be quite so bad.' The thing that crossed my mind was, 'I hope the cable doesn't snap.'

The work was hard and tough on the young boys. And seasoned miners like HARRY RADCLIFFE did their best to help them out. They understood what Bevin Boys were feeling, how unsure and out of their depth they really were.

HARRY RADCLIFFE

It must have been a terrible wrench for them to go down the pit cage for the first time. Not a thrill, although I suppose it was, in a way. But it must have been an experience, especially the first morning, going down.

Some of the Bevin Boys came from north Wales and they couldn't speak a word of English. We had one boy who was training to be a double-bass player. He was hoping to get into one of the big philharmonic orchestras, so he was very careful with his fingers. He wore gloves, whereas us boys didn't.

You had to supervise everything the Bevin Boy did. You had to make sure that his safety came first. You'd give him certain little things to do – fill the dram, make sure the place was safe, put up a post, whatever was required. That boy, well, he was your responsibility from the time the foreman handed him over till he reached the surface again.

Not all mines and people in south Wales were as friendly or supportive as Harry Radcliffe, however.

WARWICK TAYLOR

I get on very well with the Welsh people but at that particular time Bevin Boys were not really very welcome. It was understandable, because a lot of the kith and kin of mining families, their fathers or sons, were serving in the forces. We used to get a lot of stick from local people who resented us being there – quite rightly so, as they felt we'd taken the jobs away from members of their own family.

A group of Bevin Boys outside their colliery.

Despite the attitude of some of the people – and the gruelling, physical nature of the work – most of the Bevin Boys made the best of their situations. They may not have chosen to go into the mines but they could, and would, do their best.

HARVEY ALFORD

I didn't mind the work at all. I thought they were all wonderful men, the miners. I wouldn't say I enjoyed it but I didn't mind the work and the time.

I spent two years with a qualified miner, in a stall for several months. Then I spent another two years with a collier who was driving a hard heading from one part of the colliery to another, opening up a fresh seam of coal. Between us we did about ten tons of coal a day. That would be, probably, about four or five trucks. We had a set wage but the collier, if he was on what they called 'the slash' – that's piece-work in normal language – they got so much bonus over a certain amount of coal. And, if he was a good collier, he would split his overtime payment with you.

WARWICK TAYLOR

We used to get pranks and tricks played on us. Lots of the collieries had ponies underground and they'd get a Bevin Boy to take control of a pony, to move the tubs – drams, as they called them in Wales. Of course, the pony wouldn't respond. The Welsh miners would be laughing their heads off and, of course, it's obvious – the pony would only respond to a command made in Welsh!

HARVEY ALFORD

In most places, if you were in a six-foot seam there was just about half an inch clearance for my head. But when I was working in the hard heading, that was twenty feet high. I was lucky, I didn't work anywhere with water because a lot of the places were pretty wet.

You know, you even had to buy your own tools, your own shovel and pick. The only thing we were given were a pair of boots and a helmet. I had to buy kneepads because the first job I had underground was in a very low seam. When your first pair of boots wore out you had to buy a new pair.

I've got no regrets. I would have liked to have gone in the air force but I suppose, if the same thing happened again, I would do it all again. I don't suppose I'd volunteer for the mines but I don't think I'd be too upset it I was put there.

WARWICK TAYLOR

Everybody was wearing a uniform in those days and the mere fact that you were wearing civilian clothes would bring suspicion upon you. People would think you were either a deserter or a draft dodger or maybe a conscientious objector. Quite often, the local police would stop you and ask you why you weren't in uniform. You would have to show your identity card which was stamped 'Ministry of Labour, Service in Coal Mines'.

The Bevin Boys still have this stigma put on us today. A lot of people aren't fully aware that we weren't conscientious objectors. I know a lot of Bevin Boys and some have told me they actually received white feathers when they were called up because people thought, oh, they're conscientious objectors, they're afraid to go and fight. It's very sad indeed.

For people like Harvey Alford it was important to have an interest, something to do after work and on Sundays or in the evenings.

HARVEY ALFORD
    I was a keen cyclist. Tuesdays and Thursdays I would go out and do about thirty or forty miles. I had my bike sent to me soon after I got to Wales. I think that's what kept me going. I think if I hadn't been so keen on cycling I wouldn't have known what to do in the evenings.

WARWICK TAYLOR
    I regard my time in the mines as an interesting experience. Looking back now, it's one I'm glad I had and didn't miss. It taught me a lot.
    There was quite a fight to get recognition after the war. It wasn't until 1995 that the Bevin Boys were given official recognition in the form of the VE/VJ celebrations. Then in 1998 we were allowed to parade at the Cenotaph. That was a great step forward.

The Welsh collieries produced thousands of tons of coal during the war years.

HARVEY ALFORD

Three years I did in the Bevin Boys. At the end of the war in Europe I was at a big open-air party at Pentreheol near Lewistown – free teas and cakes and buns and singing and shouting. Everyone was pretty chuffed with themselves and I thought, 'Well, I'll go home now.' But we didn't. That was in the August of 1945 and I was still in the mines in '47. First in, first out. I wasn't called up until 1944. I suppose I could have picked up my goods, gone home and said, 'The war's over, I'm home. They don't want me any more.' But carry on to the bitter end, that's me.

WARWICK TAYLOR

It taught me a lot, my short time in the pits. I was only there for two years and I then managed to get into the RAF to complete my national service. What it taught me, really, was to have respect for the miner. It's a rotten job, no question about it. They were the salt of the earth – they'd never let you get into danger, always made sure you were okay.

When I got demobbed from the RAF they put a little report in my discharge papers. It said, 'This airman had completed satisfactory service in the Royal Air Force and can be highly recommended to return to his occupation as a junior clerk or coal miner.' I said to myself, 'No – I don't think so!'

'In troop convoys in those days the speed would be fifteen or sixteen knots. And in the most dangerous areas we would be zig-zagging. A convoy zig-zagging? You had to be on your toes to make sure you zigged and not zagged.'

Jim Arnold, Merchant Navy

# Conclusion

When the war finally ended in 1945 there were celebrations across the country. Bonfires were lit and crowds danced along the city streets. The sense of relief was obvious to everyone. And yet it was an occasion that was tinged with sadness and regret. Everybody knew someone who had lost family or friends – the dead would not be celebrating and, for many, it was a time simply to sit and contemplate. A Labour government was about to come into power and the sense of change hung, heavy, in the air.

BARBARA JONES

> The war changed people's outlook. It brought them out of themselves, I think. After the war, look how many women carried on working. Before the war, very few married women went out to work, and if they did, it would only be a little cleaning job or something. They got used to it during the war. I suppose they'd got used to the money and a bit of freedom. It was a big change.

Change there certainly was but, for the moment, it was time to celebrate victory in Europe and over Japan. VE Day was held on 8th May. The King and Churchill made speeches and for the crowds in London it was a time to sing and dance their way around Trafalgar Square and down the Mall. The lights were suddenly on again. Then, a few months later, on 15th August, came VJ Day. After that it was simply a case of waiting for loved ones to return.

Street party to celebrate the end of the war.

Jubilant headline on 8th May, 1945.

ESTELLE CLARKE

> When they celebrated VE Day my husband wasn't back home. He was on his way but not back yet. So we didn't have all that much to celebrate – or celebrate with. It was just a glass of mother's wine.
>
> She had this big cask of orange wine. She'd been treasuring it for when the war was over. We were all meant to sit round and celebrate. Just before VJ Day we had a terrible thunderstorm and, unfortunately, it fizzed the wine and blew the bung. It was all over the floor. So when they came home we had nothing to celebrate with.

RAY NEWBERRY

> When peace came, peace in Europe, I was on my ship in Antwerp. We were just back from the Far East and Antwerp was pretty badly knocked about. They had a huge dock area and I don't think there was one warehouse with a roof on it.

For some servicemen, coming home meant meeting children they had last seen as babies. It was a time for everyone to celebrate.

ESTELLE CLARKE

> I had been saving coupons to build up a bottom drawer for when my husband came home. Well, he was coming the next day so I had my hair in rag curlers.

And I'd got a new dress made up for my daughter. We were planning to go and meet him at the station.

In the middle of the night there was a sudden knocking on the door. My father was going to get up but my mother said, 'Stay where you are, don't answer the door.' Eventually, because the banging kept on and on, I got up – in all my glory, old pyjamas, rag curlers in my hair – and it was my husband, returned from India. And that was it for us, the big celebration.

The war was over. Hitler had been defeated and Welsh men, women and children had all played their part in the victory. Now came the task of rebuilding the country. In 1945, things looked promising. There was employment, a new National Health Service, an educational system that might just work and, shortly, would come nationalisation of the mining industry.

The future beckoned brightly. And that was how it should be. The people of Wales, along with allies world-wide, had fought for it; they deserved it. The future was theirs.

# BIBLIOGRAPHY

*War Diaries* Field Marshal Lord Alanbrook, Weidenfeld and Nicolson, 2001

*A Child's War* Mike Brown, Sutton, 2000

*Finest Hour* Tim Clayton and Phil Craig, Hodder and Stoughton, 1999

*Chronology of World War Two* Edward Davidson and Dale Manning, Cassel, 1999

*A History of Wales* John Davies, Penguin, 1993

*The 20th Century* M N Duffy, Blackwell, 1968

*Invasion* Peter Fleming, Hamish Hamilton, 1958

*Never Again* Peter Hennessy, Vintage, 1993

*Quakers in the Rhondda* Barrie Naylor, Maes yr Haf Educational Trust, 1986

*A Cardiff Family in the Forties* Malcolm Pill, Morton Priory Press, 1999

*Inferno* Vernon Scott, *The Western Telegraph*, 1980

*The Forgotten Conscript* Warwick Taylor, The Pentland Press, 2003

*They Fought in the Fields* Nicola Tyrer, Sinclair Stevenson, 1996

*London at War* Philip Ziegler, Pimlico, 2002